Table of Contents

Chapter	Beginning Page
Chapter 1	Page 1
Chapter 2	Page 10
Chapter 3	Page 20
Chapter 4	Page 36
Chapter 5	Page 52
Chapter 6	Page 62
Chapter 7	Page 74
Chapter 8	Page 88
Chapter 9	Page 103
Chapter 10	Page 118
Chapter 11	Page 132
Chapter 12	Page 146
Chapter 13	Page 164
Chapter 14	Page 179
Chapter 15	Page 198
Chapter 16	Page 213
Chapter 17	Page 225
Chapter 18	Page 244
Chapter 19	Page 260
Chapter 20	Page 275
Chapter 21	Page 289
Chapter 22	Page 305
Chapter 23	Page 320
Chapter 24	Page 332
Chapter 25	Page 343
Chapter 26	Page 356
Chapter 27	Page 369
Chapter 28	Page 380
Chapter 29	Page 392
Chapter 30	Page 405

CHAPTER 1
The World of International Economics

SUMMARY
International trade has been growing in importance in the daily economic activities of all of us. The study of international trade is critical to understanding how nations have grown, developed, and become economically powerful. While this is not a new phenomena, the exchange of goods, services, and factors has grown substantially in recent years.

Chapter 1 serves to acquaint you with the nature and characteristics of international trade. Tables 1 - 5 help demonstrate that there is an important geographic component to trade. Most of the world's trade takes place between the more highly industrialized nations and manufactured goods account for a large portion of commodity trade. The most rapid growth has occurred in several newly industrializing nations. These nations are classified as "most dynamic traders" by the World Trade Organization (Table 2).

The U.S. has an unusual position in the world trading system. The United States is the world's largest exporter and importer (Table 5) while also being less dependent on international trade than its major trading partners (Table 12). In spite of the relatively low export/GDP ratio in the U.S., the importance of international trade has been increasing rapidly since 1960. The service sector has been growing in importance in the U.S. economy and international trade in services has been a major component of trade growth.

Developing an understanding of international trade requires a specialized course because transactions take on some very special characteristics when national boundaries are involved. Trade between nations requires a greater understanding of exchange rates, differences in national policies, differences in factor mobilities, customs procedures and associated data collection, and cultural differences between nations involved in trade.

TRUE/FALSE QUESTIONS
1. In 1996, world merchandise trade reached an all time high of over $5.1 trillion.

2. The largest component of world exports (in value) is agricultural goods.

3. The developing countries dominate world trade accounting for about 70 percent of world trade in recent years.

4. The largest 10 countries are the source of almost 60% of world trade while the remaining 180 plus country traders account for just over 40% of world trade.

5. Geographically, Japan is the most important trading partner for the U.S., both in exports and imports.

6. 47% of the trade deficit of the United States in 1996 could be traced to Japan and China.

7. The capital goods category is the largest single export category and produces the largest surplus for the U.S.

8. During the 1970's, trade in services grew faster in value than merchandise trade. However, during the 1980's, exports of commercial services have grown more slowly than merchandise exports.

9. Table 12 indicates that between 1970 and 1994, most nations have increased their ratio of exports to GDP.

10. Even though a country as a whole may benefit from relative increases in international trade, individual parties or sectors may end up facing significant adjustment costs.

FILL-IN QUESTIONS

1. Considering the geographic origin of world trade, industrialized countries accounted for about _____ percent of the value of world trade in recent years.

2. The three nations with the largest share of world exports are _____, _____, and _____.

3. The three nations with the largest share of world imports are _____, _____, and _____.

4. Table 4 shows the _____ percent of North American exports are destined for Western Europe and that _____ percent of Western European exports are destined for North America.

5. The 10 largest countries are the source of almost _____ percent of world trade.

6. Considering the commodity composition of U.S. trade (Table 10), the U.S. experiences its largest deficit in the _____ category and its largest surplus in the _____ category.

7. The world's two largest exporters of services are _____ and _____ while the largest importers of services are _____ and _____.

8. Growth in the _____ ratio is an indication that a nation's economic prosperity is becoming more dependent on prosperity in the world as a whole.

9. Even though the U.S. is _____ dependent on exports than most of the industrialized countries, the relative importance of exports has _____ since 1960.

10. From table 4 it is clear that the major markets for all regions' exports are in _____, _____, and _____.

DISCUSSION QUESTIONS

1. List and discuss the characteristics that distinguish trade between two politically distinct areas from trade within a nation.

2. Using Tables 2 & 3 discuss the world's 'most dynamic traders" potential impact on the geographic structure of trade in the future.

3. Using Tables 4 & 5, discuss the importance of trade <u>among</u> industrialized nations. Suggest some reasons for the high level of concentration.

4. Table 7 suggests that trade in manufacturers accounts for over 70 percent of merchandise trade and that this percentage has grown in recent years at the expense of primary products. Compare and contrast the impact of this shift on developed and developing nations.

5. Table 9 suggests that the U.S. has its largest trade deficits with Asian nations (primarily Japan and China). Use the commodity composition of U.S. Trade data in Table 10 to explain the deficit status with these nations.

6. Trade in services was over 20 percent of world trade (approximately $1.2 trillion) by 1996. Discuss the major categories normally designated as services and some reasons for their growing importance in world trade. Why do many economists believe that the value of services is underestimated?

PROBLEMS

1. Use the information on exports and imports by region in Table 3, to find the following:

    a. The share of total export value accounted for by North America, the European Union, and Japan.

    b. The share of total import value accounted for by North America, the European Union, and Japan.

2. Table 4 presents the geographic destination of exports by region. Using this information find the following:

    a. The portion of exports that stays within each region

    b. The region that sends the largest percentage of its exports to North America

    c. The region that sends the largest percentage of its exports to Western Europe

    d. The non-Asian destination of the largest percentage of Asian exports

    e. The destination of the largest percentage of Middle Eastern exports.

3. Given the growth rates of export prices in Table 8, predict the change in price levels (increase or decrease) of the following exports:
   a. manufacturers from 1985 - 1994

   b. mining products from 1980 - 1994

   c. agricultural products from 1985 - 1994

4. Table 12 uses the ratio of exports of goods and services to GDP as a measure of the international interdependence of nations. Use this data to make the comparisons and calculations listed below. (NOTE: *simple average; it's not weighted by size of country's exports or GDP.)
   a. The average* level of interdependence for industrialized nations in 1994.

   b. The average* level of interdependence for developing nations in 1994.

   c. The average* level of interdependence of the 6 industrialized Western European nations (Belgium, France, Germany, Italy, Netherlands, U.K.) in 1994.

   d. A comparison of the average* level of interdependence between large (U.K., Germany, France) and small (Belgium, Netherlands) Western European nations in 1994.

   e. Which group of low and middle income countries has experienced the greatest growth in international interdependence between 1970 and 1994.

ANSWERS

True/False Questions
1. True
2. False
3. False
4. True
5. False
6. True
7. True
8. False
9. True
10. True

Fill-in Questions
1. 70
2. the U.S.; Germany; Japan
3. the U.S.; Germany; Japan
4. 18.9 ; 8.2
5. 60
6. consumer goods (non-auto); capital goods
7. the U.S.; France; Germany; the U.S.
8. exports/GDP
9. less; almost tripled
10. North America, Western Europe, and Asia

Problems
1. a. 16.2 + 41.2 + 8.1 = 65.5
   b. 19 + 38.8 + 6.7 = 64.5

2. a. The portion of exports that remain within a region is found by reading diagonally across the table:

Region	%
North America	36.9%
Latin America	20.2%
Western Europe	68.1%
Central/Eastern Europe	15.9%
Africa	9.7%
Middle East	9.1%
Asia	48.5%

   b. Latin America 48.4%
   c. Aside from trade within Western Europe (68.1%), Central/Eastern Europe 59.5%
   d. North America 25.9%
   e. Asia 45.6%

3. a. increase (average 1985-90, 1990-94 and 1994 all increase)
   b. decrease (changes of -2.5, -2.0, -6.0, and -3.5 would be negative)
   c. increase (changes of 7.5, -0.5, and 5.5 would be positive)

4. a. (19 + 69 + 30 + 23 + 22 + 23 + 9 + 51 + 25 + 10) / 10 = 281/10 = 28.1
   b. (7 + 28 + 24 + 52 + 12 + 30 + 39 + 36 + 13 + 22 + 27 + 177) / 12 = 38.9
   c. (69 + 23 + 22 + 23 + 51 + 25) / 6 = 35.5
   d. (25 + 22 + 23) / 3 = 23.3   <   (69 + 51) / 2 = 60
   e. East Asia and Pacific with growth from 7% to 28%

CHAPTER 2
Early Trade Theories: Mercantilism and the Transition to the Classical World of David Ricardo

SUMMARY

The Mercantilist view of economic policy came into existence in Europe between 1500 and 1750. This collection of attitudes and policies toward domestic economic activity and international trade dominated the economic thinking of the period. Mercantilist identified national wealth with the holdings of precious metals rather than a nation's productive capacity. This view of wealth and a static view of world resources led to the following policies and belief.

(1) The wealth and power of a nation - state are enhanced by acquiring precious metals.
(2) The merchant class is the most critical to the functioning of the economic system.
(3) Commodities are valued in terms of their relative labor content.
(4) A nation-state needs to maintain a positive trade balance (inflow of precious metals).
(5) Use and exchange of precious metals was severely restricted.
(6) Subsidize exports and restrict imports to maintain a positive trade balance.
(7) Encourage population growth and labor restrictions to keep wages low and productivity high.

By the late 18th century, ideas concerning international trade began to change and challenges to the Mercantilist beliefs arose. One of the first major attacks came from David Hume (1752). Hume's price-specie-flow mechanism suggested that a nation cannot maintain a positive balance of trade indefinitely. A trade surplus automatically produces internal changes in prices and wages that work to remove the surplus.

A second major assault on Mercantilism came from Adam Smith. Smith believed that a nation's wealth was reflected in its productive capacity rather than in holdings of precious metals. He objected to the extensive government controls of the Mercantilist system and believed that a government policy of laissez faire would provide the best economic environment for increasing a nation's wealth. Smith also believed that countries would gain by specializing in the production and export of commodities in which they have an absolute advantage, and importing commodities in which a trading partner has an absolute advantage.

DEFINE THE FOLLOWING KEY TERMS
absolute advantage (p. 25)

bullionism (p. 20)

favorable balance of trade or positive trade balance (p. 20)

gold standard (p. 25)

labor theory of value (p. 20)

laissez faire (p. 25)

Mercantilism (p. 19)

positive-sum game (p. 27)

price-specie-flow mechanism (p. 23)

quantity theory of money (p. 24)

unfavorable balance of trade or negative trade balance (p. 20)

zero-sum game (p. 20)

TRUE/FALSE QUESTIONS
1. David Hume and Adam Smith were strong advocates of Mercantilist policies.

2. Mercantilists believed that national wealth was reflected in a country's holdings of precious metals.

3. Mercantilist policies were designed to maintain an excess of imports over exports.

4. Mercantilists pursued policies that kept wages low.

5. Mercantilist government policies stimulated population growth by encouraging large families and financial incentives for marriage.

6. Hume's price-specie-flow mechanism argued that trade surpluses would lead to decreases in the money supply and therefore decreases in prices and wages.

7. Under a gold standard, all financial transactions must use gold as the medium of exchange.

8. Adam Smith perceived that a nation's wealth was reflected in its productive capacity.

9. In the following situation, with the labor theory of value:

	Cloth	Wheat
Germany	2 hrs./yard	4 hrs./bu.
England	4 hrs./yard	1 hr./bu.

England has an absolute advantage in cloth production.

10. Mercantilists believed that international trade was a positive-sum game.

FILL-IN QUESTIONS

1. Mercantilists viewed international trade as a _____ in which one country's economic gain was at the expense of another.

2. The Classical belief that commodities are valued relatively in terms of their relative labor content is known as the _____.

3. A country that maintains an excess of exports over imports has a _____.

4. Government policies to place strict controls on the use and exchange of precious metals are referred to as _____.

5. The relationship $M_S V = PY$ is known as the _____.

6. A system in which all currencies are pegged to gold and freely convertible into gold is known as a _____.

7. Adam Smith's belief that the role of government should be to provide an environment where individuals can pursue their own activities within the bounds of law and order and respect for property rights is known as a policy of _____.

Use the following table to answer questions 8 & 9:

Given the following table of labor requirements in two countries:

	Cars	Rice
USA	50 hrs./car	10 hrs./bu.
Japan	70 hrs./car	7 hrs./bu.

8. Japan has an absolute advantage in the production of _____.

9. The USA has an absolute advantage in the production of _____.

10. The _____ supported the control of international trade with specific policies to maximize the likelihood of a positive trade balance and resulting inflow of specie.

DISCUSSION QUESTIONS
1. Discuss the major policies of Mercantilist economic theorists.

2. Contrast the views of Adam Smith and the Mercantilists with respect to national wealth and the role of government in international trade.

3. Using Adam Smith's concept of absolute advantage, identify the basis for trade and which commodity should be exported by each country in the following case.

	Corn	Shoes
Mexico	2 hrs./bu.	4 hrs./pair
Argentina	1 hr./bu.	6 hrs./pair

4. Discuss the process by which the price-specie-flow mechanism would work to eliminate a U.S. trade surplus with Mexico given sufficient adjustment time.

PROBLEMS
Solved Problem
1. Given the following 2 country, 2 commodity case in labor hours per unit produced:

	Radios	Rubber
Thailand	10 hrs	5 hrs
Malaysia	20 hrs	2 hrs

    a. Which country has an absolute advantage in radio production?

    b. Which country has an absolute advantage in rubber production?

    c. Which commodity should Thailand export and import?

    d. Which commodity should Malaysia export and import?

Solution

    a. Thailand only takes 10 hours of labor to produce a radio compared to 20 hours in Malaysia. Thailand has an absolute advantage in radio production.

    b. Malaysia only takes 2 hours of labor to produce rubber compared to 5 hours in Thailand. Malaysia has an absolute advantage in rubber production.

    c. Thailand should export radios (their absolute advantage good) and import rubber (which can be produced more cheaply abroad.)

    d. Malaysia should export rubber (their absolute advantage good) and import radios.

2. Given a 2 country, 2 commodity world with no trade barriers.

	Exports	Imports
U.S.	$1.7 billion	$1.2 billion
Japan	$1.2 billion	$1.7 billion

    a.   Which nation has the positive trade balance?

    b.   Which nation has the negative trade balance?

According to David Hume's price-specie-flow mechanism:

    c.   Which nation will have a net inflow of specie?

    d.   Which nation will have a net outflow of specie?

    e.   Which nation will have an increase in the money supply?

    f.   Which nation will have a decrease in the money supply?

    g.   Which nation will have an increase in prices and wages?

    h.   Which nation will have a decrease in prices and wages?

    i.   Which nation will have an increase in imports and decrease in exports?

    j.   Which nation will have a decrease in imports and increase in exports?

3. Given the following 2 country, 2 commodity case in labor hours per unit produced:

	Kiwi	Boomerangs
Australia	4 hrs.	1 hr.
New Zealand	3 hrs.	2 hrs.

    a. Which country has an absolute advantage in kiwi production?

    b. Which country has an absolute advantage in boomerang production?

    c. Which commodity should Australia export and import?

    d. Which commodity should New Zealand export and import?

CASE STUDY QUESTIONS
Refer to Case Study 1 (p. 22) The Gephardt Amendment - The New Mercantilism?

    1. What actions will be taken against countries running excessive unwarranted trade surpluses with the U.S.?

    2. How do the statements by Rep. Bill Richardson (D-NM) compare to Mercantilist policies discussed in this chapter?

3. Using Hume's price-specie-flow mechanism as a guide, discuss the adjustment process resulting from a year in which "Super 301" results in the U.S. running a trade surplus with all its international trading partners.

4. Given your understanding of the concept of absolute advantage, is the statement "If we just stopped trading with the rest of the world, we'd be $100 billion ahead" correct? Why or why not?

ANSWERS
<u>True/False Questions</u>
1. False
2. True
3. False
4. True
5. True
6. False
7. False
8. True
9. False
10. False

Fill-in questions
1. zero-sum game
2. labor theory of value
3. favorable balance of trade or positive trade balance
4. bullionism
5. quantity theory of money
6. gold standard
7. laissez faire
8. rice
9. cars
10. mercantilists

Problems
2. In the 2 country, 2 commodity case involving the U.S. and Japan.
   a. In the U.S. exports (1.7 billion) exceed imports (1.2 billion) giving the U.S. a positive trade balance (5 billion).
   b. In Japan imports (1.7 billion) exceed exports (1.2 billion) giving Japan a negative trade balance (-.5 billion).

U.S.	Japan
exports > imports	exports < imports

   c. Net inflow of specie
   e. Increase in the money supply
   g. Increase in prices & wages
   i. Increase in imports and decrease in exports

   d. Net outflow of specie
   f. Decrease in money supply
   h. Decrease in prices & wages
   j. Decrease in imports & increase in exports

   UNTIL EXPORTS = IMPORTS

3. In the 2 country, 2 commodity case involving Australia and New Zealand.
   a. New Zealand only takes 3 hours to produce kiwi compared to 4 hours in Australia. New Zealand has an absolute advantage in kiwi production.

   b. Australia only takes 1 hour to produce a boomerang compared to 2 hours in New Zealand. Australia has an absolute advantage in boomerang production.

   c. Australia should export boomerangs and import kiwi.

   d. New Zealand should export kiwi and import boomerangs.

CHAPTER 3
The Classical World of David Ricardo and Comparative Advantage

SUMMARY

In Chapter 2, Adam Smith demonstrated that trade between two countries based on absolute advantage could result in benefits for both countries. While this was critical for the movement from protectionism to free trade, David Ricardo's model of comparative advantage stressed that the potential gains from international trade were not confined to absolute advantage.

Ricardo developed the concept of comparative advantage under a set of assumptions that were very restrictive and unrealistic, but these restrictions are designed to simplify the initial development of the model and will later be removed without invalidating the basic conclusions of the analysis. In order to demonstrate the strength of his theory, Ricardo chose an example in which one country (Portugal) had an absolute advantage in the production of both goods. He felt that demonstrating that Portugal could gain from trading with England would prove that the gains from trade rest on relative (comparative), not absolute, advantages.

In determining the potential for trade, Ricardo focused on relative cost differences between the two goods across the countries. While England required more labor hours to produce both wine and cloth, Ricardo points out that Portugal is relatively more efficient in the production of wine than cloth and that England's relative disadvantage is smaller in cloth. The differences in <u>relative</u> costs provide the incentive to trade. By finding an international price ratio, terms of trade, between the two countries' autarky prices, <u>both</u> countries will benefit from international trade.

Through trade, the prices of the two goods are no longer based solely on the amount of labor used in their production. Terms of trade are established by an equilibrium involving both trading countries. Trade allows each country to obtain more goods than they could using the same amount of labor time under autarky. Ricardo's model of comparative advantage reinforces the view of international trade as a positive-sum game.

While it can be demonstrated that both countries gain from international trade without altering their production of either good, Classical writers assumed that greater specialization would result from trade. Under the new international prices, a country will receive a relatively higher price for its comparative advantage good on the world market than it did in autarky. The relatively higher price will result in the devotion of more resources to the production of the comparative advantage good. At the extreme, complete specialization will occur meaning that all resources are devoted to the production of the comparative advantage good with no production of the comparative disadvantage good. Consumption remains diversified as dictated by consumer preference through trading the comparative advantage good for the comparative disadvantage good.

By including the relative resource endowments of the two countries, Production Possibility Frontiers can be used to demonstrate comparative advantage and the gains from trade.

Differences in the slopes of the PPFs (autarky price ratios) form the basis for international trade. At a terms of trade between the two autarky price ratios, each country will have a consumption possibility frontier that exceeds its PPF. The set of consumption possibilities grows as the country increases its production of its comparative advantage good. The largest potential consumption combinations for a given terms of trade occur when a nation specializes in the production of its comparative advantage good and trades for its comparative disadvantage good.

Complete specialization in both countries may be overcome by demand conditions. A country may not be large enough to satisfy world demand for its comparative advantage good, but it will still experience substantial gains from trade. The Classical writers have demonstrated that even countries with absolute advantages can benefit from trade in which some foreign goods can be purchased at prices that are relatively lower than at home. Specialization according to comparative advantage increases the efficiency with which domestic resources are used and increases the well-being of all.

DEFINE THE FOLLOWING KEY TERMS
autarky (pretrade) price ratios (p. 31)

comparative advantage (p. 31)

complete specialization (p. 35)

consumption-possibilities frontier (CPF) (p. 37)

production-possibilities frontier (PPF) (p. 36)

terms of trade (p. 31)

TRUE/FALSE QUESTIONS
1. A country with an absolute advantage in the production of a good will also have a comparative advantage in the production of that good.

2. Ricardo employs the labor theory of value in his basic model of comparative advantage.

3. Ricardo believed the basis for and gains from trade rest on comparative, not absolute, advantage.

Given the following situation, in labor hour per unit of output, answer questions 4 and 5.

	Cloth	Wheat
Germany	2 hrs./yard	1 hr./bushel
England	4 hrs./yard	3 hrs./bushel

4. Germany has an absolute advantage in cloth production.

5. England has a comparative advantage in wheat production.

6. Gains from trade result when more labor time is used to obtain the same amount of goods through trade than in autarky.

7. The closer the terms of trade are to a country's internal autarky price ratio, the greater the gain from international trade.

8. For both countries to gain, the international terms of trade must lie somewhere between the autarkic price ratios.

9. In the Classical world, a country whose production capacity of its comparative advantage good is incapable of meeting total world demand for that good will experience no gains from trade.

10. Classical writers warn that trade between developed and developing nations will prevent growth and development in the poorer nation and should be discouraged.

FILL-IN QUESTIONS

1. In the basic Ricardian model of comparative advantage, it was assumed that factors of production were _____ between alternative uses within a country.

2. In the basic Ricardian model of comparative advantage, it was assumed that factors of production were _____ between countries, that is, they _____ move between countries.

3. In the basic Ricardian model of comparative advantage, it is assumed that the market structure in the economy is characterized by _____. No single consumer or producer is large enough to influence the market; hence, all are _____.

4. While international trade can take place on the basis of absolute advantage, gains from trade on the basis of _____ can occur as well.

5. With trade between nations, prices are no longer determined solely by _____ but by an equilibrium involving the two trading countries.

6. If international trade is a positive-sum game, with trade _____ goods can be obtained for the same amount of labor time than in autarky.

7. A _____ advantage exists whenever the <u>relative</u> labor requirements differ between two commodities.

8. For both countries to gain, the international terms of trade must lie _____ the autarkic price ratios. The further the terms of trade are from the country's internal autarkic price ratio, the _____ the gain for that country from international trade.

9. The devotion of all resources to the production of one good with no production of the other good is known as _____.

10. The largest potential consumption combinations for a given terms of trade occur when a country produces only _____ and imports all of _____.

11. The theory of comparative advantage does make it clear that even if a country is absolutely more or less efficient in the production of all commodities, a basis for trade still exists if there is a difference in the _____ across commodities.

DISCUSSION QUESTIONS

1. Identify and discuss the impact of the major assumptions of the basic Ricardo model.

2. Compare and contrast the concepts of absolute and comparative advantage.

3. Develop and discuss a case in which a country has an absolute advantage in the production of a good, but does not have a comparative advantage in the production of that good.

4. Develop and discuss a case in which a country has an absolute disadvantage in the production of a good, but has a comparative advantage in the production of that good.

5. Discuss the reason that the international terms of trade will lie between the two countries' autarky terms of trade under voluntary trade.

6. Given the following example:

	Oil	Fish
Finland	2 hrs./gal	2 hrs./lb.
Belgium	6 hrs./gal	3 hrs./lb.

Identify the country with the absolute and comparative advantage in the production of each good. Choose a mutually beneficial terms of trade and discuss the potential gains from trade for each country.

7. Discuss the reason that a country would seek to establish an international terms of trade as far from their autarky price ratio as possible. What limits a country's ability to accomplish this desire?

8. Discuss the reasons that Classical writers concluded that if there is a basis for trade, it automatically leads a country to complete specialization in its comparative advantage commodity.

9. Discuss the relationship between the relative slopes of two countries' production possibility frontiers and the concept of comparative advantage.

10. Identify and discuss the static and dynamic effects of trade from the standpoint of Classical writers.

PROBLEMS

1. Given the following 2 country, 2 commodity case in labor hours per unit produced:

	javelins	pillows
Olympia	6 hrs./javelin	3 hrs./pillow
Peaceful	10 hrs./javelin	9 hrs./pillow

   a. Which country has the absolute advantage in javelin production?

   b. Which country has the absolute advantage in pillow production?

   c. Which country has the comparative advantage in javelin production?

   d. Which country has the comparative advantage in pillow production?

   e. Which country should produce and export javelins?

   f. Which country should produce and export pillows?

2. Given the following 2 country, 2 commodities case in labor hours per unit produced:

	blankets	pottery
Azteca	1 hr./blanket	1 hr./pot
Snowland	2 hr./blanket	6 hr./pot

   a. Which country has the comparative advantage in blanket production?

   b. Which country has the comparative advantage in pottery production?

   c. What is the autarky price ratio in Azteca?

   d. What is the autarky price ratio in Snowland?

   For questions 2e and 2f, assume the international terms of trade are 1 pot : 2 blankets
   e. Determine the potential gains from trade for Azteca.

   f. Determine the potential gains from trade for Snowland.

3. Using the case described in problem 2:
   a. Assume the international terms of trade are 1 blanket = 1 pot. Calculate the gains from trade for Azteca and Snowland.

   b. Assume the international terms of trade are 1 pot = 3 blankets. Calculate the gains from trade for Azteca and Snowland.

4. Given the following example in labor hours necessary to produce one unit of each commodity:

	Cars	Trucks
Fordland	14 days/car	7 days/truck
Hondia	6 days/car	6 days/truck

Assume Fordland has 70 days of labor available and Hondia has 36 days of labor available.

a. Construct a PPF for Fordland.

b. Construct a PPF for Hondia.

c. Identify the autarky price ratio in Fordland.

d. Identify the autarky price ratio in Hondia.

e. Which country has a comparative advantage in truck production?

f. Which country has a comparative advantage in car production?

CASE STUDY QUESTIONS
Refer to Case Study 1 (p. 32) Export Concentration of Selected Countries

1. Identify the nations with a comparative advantage in food and live animal production. What do these nations have in common?

2. Identify the nations with a comparative advantage in mineral fuels production? What do these nations have in common?

3. Identify the nations with a comparative advantage in machinery and manufactured items. What do these nations have in common?

4. Using Ricardo's theory of comparative advantage, identify the likely trade relations between the nations in Table 2.

5. Assume that food, live animals, and crude materials are combined in a category known as PRIMARY GOODS. Machines, transportation equipment, and basic manufactures are combined in a category known as TERTIARY GOODS.
   a. Placing tertiary goods on the vertical axis and primary goods on the horizontal axis, graph the production possibility frontiers for Japan and Cuba.

   b. What do the relative slopes demonstrate about comparative advantage?

   c. Who would be expected to export and import each group of products?

   d. Given the relative size of the two economies, would you expect complete specialization in a two country trading relationship.

   e. From the Classical perspective, should Cuba trade with Japan? If so, what are the potential gains?

ANSWERS

True/False Questions
1. False
2. True
3. True
4. True
5. False
6. False
7. False
8. True
9. False
10. False

Fill-in questions
1. completely mobile
2. completely immobile; do not
3. perfect competition; price takers
4. comparative
5. the labor theory of value
6. more
7. comparative advantage
8. somewhere between; greater
9. complete specialization
10. its comparative advantage good; its comparative disadvantage good.
11. degree of <u>relative</u> efficiency

Problems
1. a. Olympia has an absolute advantage in javelin production, 6 hrs./10 hrs.
   b. Olympia has an absolute advantage in pillow production, 3 hrs./9 hrs.
   c. Peaceful has a comparative advantage in javelin production, (Peaceful's 1J:10/9P < Olympia's 1J:2P   least disadvantage).
   d. Olympia has a comparative advantage in pillow production, (Olympia's 1P:1/2J < Peaceful's 1P:9/10J   greatest advantage).
   e. Peaceful should produce and export its comparative advantage product.
   f. Olympia should produce and export its comparative advantage product.

2. a. Snowland has a comparative advantage in blanket production (Snowland's 1 blanket:1/3 pot < Azteca's 1 blanket:1 pot   least disadvantage).
   b. Azteca has a comparative advantage in pottery production (Azteca's 1 pot:1blanket < Snowland's 1 pot:3 blankets   greatest advantage).
   c. autarky price ratio 1 blanket : 1 pot or 1 pot : 1 blanket
   d. autarky price ratio 1 blanket : 1/3 pot or 1 pot : 3 blankets

e. Azteca trades 1 pot for 2 blankets. It takes 1 hour to make 1 pot (direct cost) and would take 2 hours to make 2 blankets (indirect cost). Azteca saves 1 hour of labor per pot exported (2 hrs - 1 hr = 1 hr).
f. Snowland trades 2 blankets for 1 pot. It takes 4 hours to make 2 blankets (direct cost) and would take 6 hours to make 1 pot (indirect cost). Snowland saves 2 hours of labor per pot imported (6 hrs - 4 hrs = 2 hrs).

Both nations gain from trade.

3. a. The international terms of trade are the same as Azteca's autarky price ratio. Under this circumstance all of the gains will accrue to Snowland. Snowland trades 1 blanket for 1 pot. The blanket takes 2 hours to produce (direct cost) and the pot would have taken 6 hours to produce (indirect cost). Snowland saves 4 hours per pot imported (6 hrs - 2 hrs = 4 hrs).
b. The international terms of trade are the same as Snowland's autarky price ratio. Under this circumstance all of the gains will accrue to Azteca. Azteca trades pot for 3 blankets. The pot takes 1 hour to produce (direct cost) and the 3 blankets would have taken 3 hours to produce (indirect cost). Azteca saves 2 hours per pot exported (3 hrs - 1 hr = 2 hrs).

4. a. If Fordland completely specializes in truck production, they could use their 70 days of labor to produce 10 trucks (70 days/7 days per truck). If Fordland completely specializes in car production, they could use their 70 days of labor to produce 5 cars (70 days/14 days per car). In graphical terms:

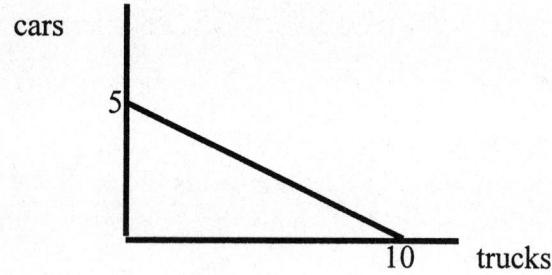

b. If Hondia completely specializes in truck production, they could use their 36 days of labor to produce 6 trucks (36 days/6 days per truck). If Hondia completely specializes in car production, they could use their 36 days of labor to produce 6 cars (36 days/6 days per car). In graphical terms:

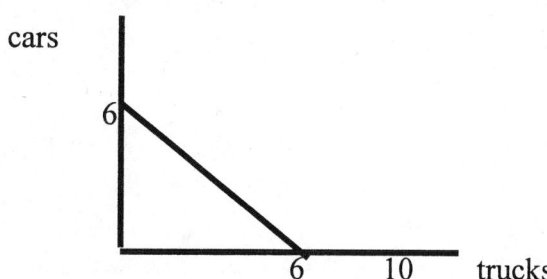

The two PPFs are straight lines (rather than bowed out) because of the assumption of constant costs of production.

c. The slopes of the two PPFs (ignoring the negative sign) are each country's autarky price ratios. In Fordland, the autarky price ratio is 1 truck : .5 car.

d. In Hondia, the autarky price ratio is 1 truck : 1 car. The differences in these price ratios form the basis of trade.

e. Given that Fordland has an opportunity cost of .5 cars : truck relative to 1 car : truck in Hondia, Fordland has a comparative advantage in truck production.

f. Given that Hondia has an opportunity cost of 1 truck : car relative to 2 trucks : car in Fordland, Hondia has a comparative advantage in car production.

CHAPTER 4
Extensions and Tests of the Classical Model of Trade

SUMMARY
The Ricardian model of Comparative Advantage discussed in Chapter 3 was developed under a series of very restrictive assumptions. Chapter 4 demonstrates the power of the concept by analyzing the impact of the relaxation of these assumptions.

The first assumption to be relaxed moves the model beyond the labor theory of value to monetary values of commodities. This extension requires a set of money prices in each country's currency and an exchange rate for comparisons. The exchange rate allows the value of all goods to be stated in terms of one currency. In this monetized version of the comparative advantage model, a country is designated to export a good when it can produce the good the most inexpensively, given wage rates and the exchange rate.

The second assumption to be relaxed moves the model beyond the two commodity setting to multiple commodities. With more than two commodities, the goods are arranged by their relative labor requirements. The goods are compared to the relative wage cost of the two countries and a country exports the products whose relative labor requirements are less than the relative wage cost. Goods with a relative labor requirement greater than the relative wage cost should be imported and in cases where the relative labor requirement is exactly equal to the relative wage rate, the goods may not be traded. The multiple commodity model of comparative advantage can be used to examine changes in wage rates, the exchange rate, preferences, and the level of technology (the Dornbusch-Fischer-Samuelson model).

The third assumption to be relaxed allows for the existence of transportation costs. The addition of transportation costs does not impact the general workings of the comparative advantage model, but it does result in some nontraded goods. When the cost of transporting goods from one country to the next exceeds the cost advantages, the good will not be traded.

The fourth assumption to be relaxed moves the model beyond a two country framework to explore multiple countries. The addition of a third country to the model results in a "middle country" in the analysis. The pattern of trade is clear between the two countries with the greatest difference between their autarky prices. The direction of trade for the middle country will depend on the international terms of trade. While the addition of multiple countries adds some potential ambiguity to the model, the basic results of the model hold up very well to the relaxation of Ricardo's restrictive assumptions.

Empirical analysis of the relationship between relative labor productivity, relative wages, and the structure of exports have supported the Classical model of comparative advantage. The work of MacDougall in the 1950s suggested that export performance was consistent with relative labor productivity and wage rates. Golub used 1990 data to examine the association between unit labor costs by individual industries and trade performance. The Golub analysis also suggests the Classical model is generally consistent with observed trading patterns.

DEFINE THE FOLLOWING KEY TERMS
boundary good (p. 49)

exchange rate (p. 43)

exchange rate limits (p. 45)

export condition (p. 44)

nontraded goods (p. 54)

tradable goods (p. 53)

unit labor costs (p. 56)

wage rate limits (p. 43)

TRUE/FALSE QUESTIONS
1. The exchange rate is the number of units of one currency that exchange for one unit of a second currency.

2. If international terms of trade do not produce balanced trade in a two country, two commodity model with monetary prices, the price-specie-flow mechanism will contribute to the growing trade imbalance.

3. In the 2 country monetized version of the Classical model, the export condition can be expressed as
$$a_{1j} W_1 e < a_{2j} W_2 \text{ or}$$

$a_{1j}/a_{2j} < W_1 \cdot W_2/e$.

4. The Ricardian model of comparative advantage has proven very robust in a multicommodity setting.

Assuming Agra is country 1 and Manku is country 2, answer Questions 5-7 with the following ranking of commodities according to their relative labor requirements (a_1/a_2):

<u>Coffee</u>	<u>Iron</u>	<u>Chocolate</u>	<u>W_2W_1e</u>	<u>Cars</u>	<u>Pens</u>
3/2	8/4	6/2	4/[2(.5/1)]	15/3	6/1.

5. Agra should export coffee and pens and import iron and cars.

6. Manku should export cars and pens and import coffee, iron, and chocolate.

7. Chocolate is the boundary good in this example.

8. A good can be classified as both tradable and nontraded.

9. In his 1951 analysis, MacDougall found that the U.S. and U.K. were similar enough in structure to have comparative advantages in the production of the same goods.

10. The Classical model provides a clear indication that government constraints and reallocative taxes on industry increase economic development and the gains from trade.

FILL-IN QUESTIONS

1. Monetization in the Classical model is accomplished by establishing a domestic value of each good equal to labor requirement per unit x _____.

2. If $a_{1coffee} W_1 e < a_{2coffee} W_2$, country _____ should export coffee and country _____ should import coffee.

3. Given the <u>wage levels in both countries</u>, the end points of the range within which the exchange rate can vary without eliminating the basis for trade are known as _____.

4. Given the <u>exchange rate and one wage</u>, the end points of the range within which the _____ can vary without eliminating the basis for trade are known as the wage rate limits.

5. In a multiple commodity model of comparative advantage, the goods are ranked in ascending order according to _____.

6. In the multiple country model of comparative advantage, the incentive for trade will be the <u>greatest</u> between the two countries with the _____.

7. In a Classical model with multiple commodities, changes in the _____ and the _____ will change comparative advantages and a country's ability to export and import.

8. The cost associated with moving a product from one country's location to another is known as the _____.

9. When the comparative advantage in the production of a good is overcome by the cost of transportation the good will tend to be a _____.

10. The Classical model indicates that government restraints and taxes on industry _____ economic competitiveness and _____ the gains from trade.

DISCUSSION QUESTIONS

1. Discuss the determination of the export condition in the monetized Classical model. Explain the determination of the wage rate limits for one of the two countries. Explain the determination of the exchanges rate limits.

2. In the multiple commodity setting for the Classical model, discuss the importance of ordering the commodities on the analysis. Examine the impact of an increase in the relative wages in one of the two countries. Explain the impact of a change in the exchange rate.

3. Discuss the concept of a boundary good in the Dornbusch-Fischer-Samuelson model. Will the boundary good be traded? Why or why not? Explain the factors that could lead to a change in the boundary good.

4. Coffee is classified as a tradable good in Peru. Explain the conditions that could lead coffee to also be a nontraded good.

5. In a three country model of comparative advantage, discuss the existence of a "middle country" in the analysis. How is the middle country's ability to export related to the international terms of trade?

6. Summarize MacDougall's 1951 empirical test of comparative advantage using the U.S. and U.K. Discuss the 10 goods that you would choose to replicate the study today using the U.S. and Japan.

PROBLEMS

1. Given the following information:

	Wage/hr.	Cars Labor/unit	Price	Shirts Labor/unit	Price
U.S.	$10/hr	10 hrs/car	$100	3 hrs/shirt	$30
Mexico	2 pesos/h	30 hrs/car	60p	5 hrs/shirt	10p

   a. Which country has an absolute advantage in the production of both goods?

   b. Given an exchange rate of $1 = 2p, determine the comparative advantages.

   c. Using the export condition, determine which nation will export cars.

   d. Using the export condition, determine which nation will export shirts.

   e. Using the $1 = 2p exchange rate and the $10 per hour U.S. wage rate, determine the wage rate limits for Mexico.

   f. Using the $1 = 2p exchange rate and the 2p per hour Mexican wage rate, determine the wage rate limits for the U.S.

   g. Using the $10 per hour U.S. wage rate and the 2p per hour Mexican wage rate, determine the exchange rate limits.

2. Given the following example of multiple commodities in a comparative advantage model.

	Wage	Wheat	Apples	Pecans	Forks	Plates	Glasses
Hong Kong	8HK/hr.	1	2	3	3	8	2
New Zealand	2NZ/hr.	2	3	4	10	20	6

    a.   Place the commodities in order of ascending relative labor requirements.

    b.   Using an exchange rate of 2 Hong Kong (HK) = 1 New Zealand (NZ), locate the relative wage cost.

    c.   Determine the exports and imports for both nations.

    d.   Examine the impact of an increase in Hong Kong's wages to 9HK/hr.

    e.   With Hong Kong's new wage of 9HK/hr, examine the impact of a change in the exchange rate to 3HK = 1NZ.

3. Given the following information:

	Wage/hr.	Soft Drinks Labor/unit	Price	Chocolate Labor/unit	Price
Cola	1 RD/hr	1 hrs/drink	1 RD	2 hrs/bar	2 RD
Choca	1 Hersher/hr	2 hrs/drink	2 Hersher	3 hrs/bar	3 Hersher

    a. Which country has an absolute advantage in the production of the two goods.

    b. Given an exchange rate of 1 Hersher = .6 RD, determine comparative advantages.

    c. Using the export conditions, determine which nation will export each good.

    d. Examine the impact of the addition of a one labor hour per unit cost of transportation for exports.

4. In the following 3 country model:

Country	Steel	Toys	Autarky Price Ratio
China	2 hrs/ton	4 hrs/unit	1 toy: 2 steel
Italy	2 hrs/ton	6 hrs/unit	1 toy: 3 steel
Brazil	3 hrs/ton	12 hrs/unit	1 toy: 4 steel

a. Which two countries have the greatest incentive for trade?

b. Which country has the comparative advantage for steel?

c. Which country has the comparative advantage for toys?

d. What are the boundaries for the international terms of trade?

e. What terms of trade would result in the middle country having no potential gains from trade?

f. What terms of trade would result in the middle country exporting toys and importing steel?

g. What terms of trade would result in the middle country exporting steel and importing toys?

CASE STUDY QUESTIONS
Refer to Case Study 1 (p. 53) The Size of Transportation Cost

1. If imports are assumed to be on average 10% cheaper than domestically produced goods, use the table to determine which nations will no longer find it advantageous to import in 1975, 1985 and 1995.

2. Of the four goods listed in the Commodity: Route table, which is most likely to fall from the status of traded to nontraded good because of high transportation cost? Is this good still tradable?

3. Assume a new cargo airplane is developed and it reduces transportation costs by 50 percent. Explain the impact on international trade.

4. A scientist is hired to develop a synthetic substitute for jute in Europe. Does she need to produce the product at a cost below that of jute in Bangladesh in order to be successful in the European market? Why or why not?

Refer to Case Study 2 (p. 57) Labor Productivity and Import Penetration in the U.S. Steel Industry

1. Using the unit labor cost figures provided, determine which nations are most likely to export iron and steel in 1972, 1977, and 1982. Which nations are most likely to be importers?

2. Explain shifts from exporter to importer (or vice-versa) using the changes in productivity and wages.

3. Using the graphs of labor productivity and import penetration, discuss the impact of changes in labor productivity on import penetration for the years 1973-1977, 1978-1982, 1982-1987.

4. Given the relationship discussed in question 3, discuss some reasons for the trends in U.S. productivity and your suggestions for decreasing import penetration in iron and steel.

ANSWERS

True/False Questions
1. True
2. False
3. False
4. True
5. False
6. True
7. False
8. True
9. False
10. False

Fill-in Questions
1. the country's wage rate
2. 1; 2
3. exchange rate; exchange rate limits
4. other country's wage rate; wage rate limits
5. their relative labor requirements
6. greatest difference in autarky prices
7. wage rates; the exchange rate
8. transportation cost
9. nontraded good
10. reduce; reduce

Problems
1. a. U.S. has an absolute advantage in both
   b. The U.S. has a comparative advantage in cars and Mexico has a comparative advantage in shirts.

   c. $a_{1j} W_1 e < a_{2j} W_2$
      10 hrs x $10 x $1/2p < 30 x 2p
      $100 x $1/2p < 60p
      50p < 60p
      The U.S. will export cars.

   d. 3 hrs x $10 x $1/2p > 5 hrs x 2p
      $30 x $1/2p > 10p
      15p > 10p
      Mexico will export shirts.

e. $a_{1j}/a_{2j} = W_2/(W_1 \times e)$
   $10/30 = W_2/(\$10 \times 1/2)$ $3/5 = W_2/(\$10 \times 1/2)$
   $1/3 = W_2/5p$ $3/5 = W_2/\$5p$
   $W_2 = 5/3$ $W_2 = 3p$
   wage limits for Mexico are 1 2/3 p/hr. and 3 p/hr.

f. $10/30 = 2/(W_1 \times 1/2)$ $3/5 = 2/W_1 \times 1/2$
   $1/3 = 4/W_1$ $3/5 = 4/W_1$
   $12 = W_1$ $20/3 = W_1$
   wage limits for the U.S. are $12 per hr. and $6 2/3 per hr.

g. $10/30 = 2/\$10 \times e$ $3/5 = 2/10 \times e$
   $1/3 = 1/5e$ $3/5 = 1/5e$
   $5/3 = 1/e$ $15/5 = 1/e$
   $3/5 = e$ $1/3 = e$
   the exchange rate limits are $1 = 3p and $3 = 5p

2. a.
	Forks	Glasses	Plates	Wheat	Apples	Pecans
	3	2	8	1	2	3
	10	6	20	2	3	4

b. $W_2 / W_1 e$
   NZ/hr / (8HK/hr x 1NZ/2HK)
   2 / 4
   relative wage cost = $W_2/W_1 e = 1/2$

c. Hong Kong will export Forks, Glasses, Plates and import Apples and Pecans. New Zealand will export Apples and Pecans and import Forks, Glasses, and Plates. Wheat is a boundary good.

d. $2/(9 \times 1/2) = 4/9 < 1/2$
   Hong Kong continues to export Forks, Glasses, and Plates.
   New Zealand now exports Pecans, Apples, and Wheat.

e. $2/(9 \times 1/3) = 2/3 > 4/9$
   Hong Kong now exports Forks, Glasses, Plates, and Wheat. New Zealand now exports Pecans. Apples are now a boundary good.

3. a. Cola has the absolute advantage in both goods.

   b. Prices in RDs:

	Soft Drinks	Chocolate
Cola	1 RD/drink	2 RD/bar
Choca	1.2 RD/drink	1.8 RD/bar

Cola has the comparative advantage in soft drinks.
Choca has the comparative advantage in chocolate.

    c. $a_{1j} W_1 e < a_{2j} W_2$
1 hr. x 1 RD x 1/6 < 2 hr. x 1H
1.67 < 2
Cola should export soft drinks

2 x 1 RD x 1.67 > 3 x 1
3.34 > 3
Choca should export chocolate bars

    d. $(a_{1j} + tr_2)/a_{2j} < W_2/(W_1 \times e)$ export condition
(1 + 1) / 2 > 1/1 x 1.67
1 > .6
Cola will no longer export soft drinks

export condition $W_2/(W_1 \times e) < a_{1j}/(a_{2j} + tr_j)$
1/(1 x 1.67) > 2/(3 + 1)
.6 > 2/4
.6 > .5
Choca will no longer export chocolate bars

While both are tradable goods, the existence of transportation costs result in their becoming nontraded goods.

4.   a.   China and Brazil have the greatest incentive for trade because they have the greatest difference between their autarky prices.

    b.   Brazil has the greatest comparative advantage in steel. (4/12 < 2/3)

    c.   China has the greatest CA in toys (12/4 > 3/2)

    d.   The international terms of trade will fall between the two autarky price ratios of 1 toy:2 steel and 1 toy:4 steel.

    e.   If the terms of trade are 1 toy:3 steel, Italy will have no potential gains from trade.

    f.   If the terms of trade are 1 toy:more than 3 steel, Italy will export toys and import steel.

    g.   If the terms of trade are 1 toy:less than 3 steel, Italy will export steel and import toys.

CHAPTER 5
Introduction to Neoclassical Trade Theory: Tools to be Employed

SUMMARY

This chapter is designed to review some of the neoclassical tools that will be used to analyze the impact of trade. The review begins with the theory of consumer behavior, moves into production theory, and finishes with a review of production possibility frontiers.

In terms of consumer behavior, consumers seek to maximize their satisfaction subject to their budget constraints. Consumer satisfaction is measured using consumer indifference curves. Each curve represents a combination of points representing bundles of goods that bring the consumer the same level of satisfaction. The indifference curves are downward sloping, convex to the origin, never intersect, and represent higher levels of satisfaction as they move further from the origin.

When the concern turns to the entire country rather than an individual, community indifference curves are used. Community indifference curves show the various consumption combinations of two goods that yield equivalent satisfaction for the country. The use of community indifference curves is complicated by the fact that the curve is drawn for a particular income distribution and changes in that distribution will change the indifference curves.

The constraint on the consumer is the available income or the budget constraint. The consumer maximizes satisfaction when the budget line just touches the highest indifference curve attainable. This point represents the combination of goods that provides the greatest satisfaction available for the amount of income to be spent. This is the consumer equilibrium.

From the standpoint of production, the focus will be on input choice and production efficiency. Isoquants are used to relate output to the factor inputs (K and L). Each isoquant shows the various combinations of inputs that produce the same level of output. The shape of the isoquant is determined by the ease of substitutability of one input for the other. Isoquants are downward sloping, nonintersecting, and represent a particular level of output. The firm must also know the relative cost of the inputs in order to choose a production combination. An isocost line shows the various combinations of factors that can be purchased for a given total cost at given factor prices. The point at which the isocost curve is tangent to the highest possible isoquant is the point of producer equilibrium. The firm is obtaining the maximum output for a given cost.

Two final concepts are used to examine the entire economy. They are the Edgeworth box diagram and the production possibilities frontier. The Edgeworth box takes the isoquants of two different firms (assumed to be the only two industries in the economy) and combines them in one diagram. The points of tangency between the isoquants of the two firms form the production efficiency locus. The points along this locus represent the maximum output combinations of the two goods from the available factors of production and are efficient.

The production possibility frontier (PPF) represents the maximum combinations of output that can be produced with given resources and the current technology. The typical PPF is drawn concave to the origin representing increasing opportunity costs associated with producing more of a particular good. This is often related to "specific factors" in the sense that the most adaptable factors are moved into an industry first. As production increases, less adaptable factors are used and the opportunity cost rises. The true analytical source of the PPF is the production efficiency locus from the Edgeworth box. The PPF and the production efficiency locus are both made up of points that require a decrease in the production of one good in order to increase the production of the other good. All resources are employed in their most efficient manner given technology and the shape and position reflect the endowments of capital and labor in the economy.

DEFINE THE FOLLOWING KEY TERMS
budget constraint (or budget line) (p. 69)

cardinal utility (p. 63)

community indifference curve (or country indifference curve) (p. 67)

constant returns to scale (p. 74)

consumer equilibrium (p. 70)

consumer indifference curve (p. 63)

decreasing returns to scale (p. 74)

diminishing marginal rate of substitution (p. 65)

Edgeworth box diagram (p. 77)

homotheticity (p. 74)

increasing opportunity costs (p. 79)

increasing returns to scale (p. 74)

isocost line (p. 74)

isoquant (p. 73)

marginal physical product (p. 74)

marginal rate of technical substitution (p. 74)

marginal rate of transformation (p. 80)

marginal utility (p. 65)

ordinal utility (p. 63)

Pareto efficiency (p. 79)

producer equilibrium (p. 76)

production efficiency locus (p. 79)

transitivity (p. 64)

TRUE/FALSE QUESTIONS

1. In drawing consumer indifference curves, micro theory uses the concept of cardinal utility, which means that actual numerical values can be attached to welfare.

2. The reason for convexity of indifference curves lies in the economic principle of diminishing marginal utility.

3. To obtain the community indifference curve, the individual indifference curves of all citizens are summed horizontally.

4. The tangency between an indifference curve and a budget constraint provides the point of consumer equilibrium.

5. An isoquant shows the various combinations of two inputs that produce the same level of output.

6. If an isoquant is drawn as a right angle, easy substitution of one factor for another is possible.

7. An isocost line shows the various combinations of output that can be produced for the same total cost.

8. At the point of producer equilibrium, the firm is obtaining maximum output for a given cost.

9. Points of Pareto efficiency are efficient because it is necessary to give up output of one good in order to increase the production of the other.

10. A convex production possibilities frontier demonstrates increasing opportunity costs.

FILL-IN QUESTIONS

1. Given transitivity, if bundle B_2 is preferred to bundle B_1 and bundle B_3 is preferred to bundle B_2, the bundle B_3 _____ to bundle B_1.

2. The _____ is the name given to reflect the slope of the indifference curve.

3. Indifference curves used to represent the welfare of the country rather than an individual are known as _____.

4. A _____ is used to examine the income level of a particular consumer.

5. At the point of consumer equilibrium, the equilibrium condition that MU_x/MU_y = _____ is satisfied.

6. In production theory, _____ means that the slope of all isoquants is the same when moving along a ray from the origin.

7. If all the inputs are changed by a given percentage, then output will change in the same direction by the same percentage if the production function is characterized by _____.

8. An _____ takes the isoquants of two industries and combines them into a single diagram.

9. The line that connects the points of tangency in an Edgeworth box is known as the _____.

10. The formal name for the (negative of the) slope of the PPF is the _____.

DISCUSSION QUESTIONS

1. Discuss the characteristics of consumer indifference curves and community indifference curves. Why is the use of indifference curves to represent community welfare a more complex phenomenon than representing individual welfare.

2. At point A, $MU_x/P_x > MU_y/P_y$. Is A the point of consumer equilibrium? Why or why not?

3. At point C, $MPP_L/W = MPP_k/r$. Is C the point of consumer equilibrium? Why or why not?

4. Explain why points on the production efficiency locus are Pareto efficient.

5. Discuss the three explanations for the concave shape of the PPF. How is the shape related to production efficiency?

PROBLEMS

1. Use Figure 1 on page 65 to answer the following questions:

   a. What is the relationship between points F and H?

   b. What is the relationship between points F and J?

   c. What is the relationship between points F and G?

   d. What is the relationship between points G and J?

   e. What is the relationship between points K and G?

2. At the current level of consumption:
   $MU_x = 20$
   $MU_y = 15$
   $P_x = 2$
   $P_y = 3$.

   a. Is the consumer currently at equilibrium?

   b. Is there an adjustment that would increase the consumer's satisfaction?

3. At the current level of production:
   $MPP_L = 20$
   $MPP_k = 20$
   $w = \$5$
   $r = \$10$

   a. Is the current level of production a point of producer equilibrium?

   b. Is there an adjustment that would increase production efficiency?

CASE STUDY QUESTIONS
Refer to Case Study 1 (p.72) Consumer Expenditure Patterns in the United States

1. Of the three broad categories of goods and services (durable goods, nondurable goods, services) which have shown steady growth over the last 35 years? Which have declined?

2. Identify the one item within each category that has shown the steadiest growth over the time period.

3. Given the expectation of continued income growth over the next 2-3 decades, which industries would offer the best growth potential? Which industries should be avoided?

ANSWERS

True/False Questions
1. False
2. False
3. False
4. True
5. True
6. False
7. False
8. True
9. True
10. False

Fill-in questions
1. is preferred
2. marginal rate of substitution
3. community indifference curves or country indifference curves
4. budget constraint or budget line
5. P_x/P_y
6. homotheticity
7. constant returns to scale
8. Edgeworth box
9. production efficiency locus or contract curve
10. marginal rate of transformation

Problems
1. a. indifferent between F and H
   b. J is preferred to F
   c. indifferent between F and G
   d. J is preferred to G
   e. G is preferred to K

2. a. No, 20/2 > 15/5
   b. consumption of good X should increase and good Y should be decreased.

3. a. No, 20/$5 > 20/$10
   b. the producer has the incentive to employ more labor and less capital services.

CHAPTER 6
Gains from Trade in Neoclassical Theory

SUMMARY

This chapter will use the microeconomic tools developed in Chapter 5 to update the Ricardian analysis by introducing increasing opportunity costs, factors of production other than labor, and explicit demand considerations. The economy is assumed to be seeking to maximize welfare through the behavior of its economic agents. Additional assumptions include:

(1) consumers seek to maximize satisfaction.
(2) workers seek to maximize returns from productive activity.
(3) factors are mobile within a country but not between countries.
(4) no transportation costs or trade barriers exist.
(5) perfect competition exists.

The analysis begins with autarky which is the total absence of participation in international trade. Using a PPF, the point of production equilibrium is the tangency between the PPF and the relative price line. In the absence of trade, the point of production is also the point of consumption. To obtain general equilibrium, the production point on the PPF must be tangent to both the relative price line and a consumer indifference curve. This point would be autarky equilibrium for the economy as a whole.

The opening of the economy to trade introduces a new set of relative prices. These new prices force a reallocation of production and consumption patterns. The new prices represent a relative increase in the price of one good and a relative decrease in the other. This difference indicates that the home country is relatively more efficient in producing the first good and relatively less efficient in producing the second. This realization will lead to increases in the production of the first good and decreases in the production of the second. The new production point will be at the tangency between the PPF and the new price line.

Another change is that the nation is no longer forced to produce and consume at the same point. At the new prices, the country can exchange units of the first good for units of the second to reach to point of consumption efficiency. Consumer equilibrium occurs at the tangency of the new price line and the consumer indifference curve. This consumption point is beyond the PPF representing the gains from trade (see Figure 3).

In a two country world with two goods (X and Y), the process of trade can be demonstrated. To facilitate trade the home country has a comparative advantage in good X while the partner country has a comparative advantage in good Y. Faced with the new international prices, each country has an incentive to produce more of its comparative advantage good. Trade allows each country to export its comparative advantage good at a relatively higher price and purchase its comparative disadvantage good for a relatively lower price. The trade moves each country to a point of consumer equilibrium beyond the PPF. In Figure 5, it is obvious that both countries gain from trade.

The examination of the minimum conditions for trade focuses on differences in supply conditions and differences in demand conditions. In the neoclassical model two countries with identical PPFs can benefit from trade if different demand conditions exist with the presence of increasing opportunity costs. The differences in demand produce differences in relative prices and autarky production points. Trade brings about a new set of relative prices and the opportunity for each country to increase the production of its comparative advantage good. Each country trades its comparative advantage good and receives its comparative disadvantage good in order to reach a point of consumer equilibrium on a higher indifference curve. In spite of the two countries having identical PPFs, gains from trade were possible.

The second situation considers two countries with different production conditions but the same demand conditions. Each country will have its own PPF to represent the different production conditions, but the two will share the same set of indifference curves. The new international prices encourage each country to increase the production of its comparative advantage good. Through trade each can export its comparative advantage good and consume more of the comparative disadvantage good through imports. The point of consumer equilibrium is the same for both countries (given identical demand conditions) and represents increased welfare for both countries. In spite of the common demand conditions, both countries gain from trade.

There are three additional assumptions that were important in this analysis. These assumptions are costless factor mobility, full employment of resources, and community indifference curves that actually show welfare changes. While the assumptions may not be an accurate portrayal of the real world, these models still demonstrate the potential gains from international trade.

DEFINE THE FOLLOWING KEY TERMS
compensation principle (p. 99)

consumption gain (or gains from exchange) (p. 92)

production gain (or gains from specialization) (p. 92)

total gains from trade (p. 92)

trade adjustment assistance (p. 99)

trade triangle (p. 91)

trading line (p. 90)

TRUE/FALSE QUESTIONS
1. In autarky, the point of production is necessarily the consumption point as well.

2. The relative price line that is tangent to the country's PPF is also the country's trading line.

3. The consumption gains from trade refer to the incentive to produce more of the comparative advantage good as a result of the new prices.

4. A basis for trade exists whenever the relative prices of the two goods in the two potential trading partners are the same.

5. The two principal conditions for two countries with identical PPFs to benefit from trade are differences in demand conditions and the presence of increasing opportunity costs.

6. Two nations with identical production conditions would share the same community indifference curve map.

7. The gains from trade are shown graphically as a movement up and left along a particular community indifference curve.

8. The point of consumer equilibrium after trade is the tangency between the international price line and the community indifference curve.

9. The underlying basis for trade can change as technology changes or as factors move between countries.

10. To draw conclusions about improvements in welfare as a result of trade, the following conditions are pertinent: (a) individuals in the economy have different tastes, and (b) the opening of the economy to trade radically alters the distribution of income.

FILL-IN QUESTIONS

1. _____ means the total absence of participation in international trade.

2. The point at which MRT = MC_x/MC_y = P_x/P_y = MU_x/MU_y = MRS is the point of _____ for the economy as a whole.

3. The trade pattern represented by a nations exports, a nation's imports, and the trading line is known as the _____.

4. The combination of the gains from exchange and the gains from specialization are known as the _____.

5. Theoretically, the two principal sources of relative price variation between two countries are _____ and _____.

6. In the case of two nations with different production conditions, if the nations share similar technologies, the relative availability of the factors must _____.

7. A U.S. program designed to help in the transition following tariff reductions through trade negotiations is known as _____.

8. Changes in the distribution of income as a result of opening the economy to trade can cause the _____ to intersect.

9. The _____ concludes that potential gains from trade exist in the sense that, within the country, the people who gain from trade can compensate the losers and still be better off.

10. When two countries have identical demand conditions, the minimal condition for gains from international trade is a difference in _____.

DISCUSSION QUESTIONS

1. Discuss the conditions for producer and consumer equilibrium in the autarky model. Why must the consumption possibility frontier and the production possibility frontier be identical?

2. As a result of trade, the country is exposed to a new set of relative prices. Discuss the production and consumption adjustments that result from facing the new prices.

3. Using the neoclassical model, discuss the gains from trade and the use of the trade triangle to summarize the pattern of trade.

4. Discuss the minimum conditions necessary for generating relative price differences in autarky between two nations.

5. Demonstrate the potential gains from trade between two nations with identical demand conditions.

6. Demonstrate the potential gains from trade between two nations with identical production conditions.

7. Discuss the assumptions that are made in order to analyze the potential gains from trade between nations.

PROBLEMS

1. Use Figure 3 on page 90 to identify the following:
   a. the autarky price ratio

   b. autarky production of good X

   c. autarky production of good Y

   d. autarky consumption of good X

   e. autarky consumption of good Y

   f. new price ratio with the opening of trade

   g. production point with trade

   h. post-trade production of good X

   i. post-trade production of good Y

   j. consumption point with trade

   k. post-trade consumption of good X

   l. post-trade consumption of good Y

   m. trade triangle

   n. pre-trade level of welfare

   o. post-trade level of welfare

2. Use Figure 8 on page 97 to identify the following:
   a. country I's comparative advantage good

   b. country I's autarky price ratio

   c. country I's autarky production point

   d. country II's comparative advantage good

   e. country II's autarky price ratio

   f. country II's autarky production point

   g. the international terms of trade

   h. country I's post-trade production point

   i. country I's post-trade production of good X

   j. country I's post-trade production of good Y

   k. country I's post-trade consumption point

   l. country I's post-trade consumption of good X

   m. country I's post-trade consumption of good Y

   n. country II's post-trade production point

   o. country II's post-trade production of good X

p.   country II's post-trade production of good Y

q.   country II's post-trade consumption point

r.   country II's post-trade consumption of good X

s.   country II's post-trade consumption of good Y

t.   post-trade level of welfare for both nations

CASE STUDY QUESTIONS
Refer to Case Study 1 (p.100) Income Distribution Change with Increased Trade in the U.S.

1.   Discuss the impact of trade on the demand for productive inputs. How will these changes impact income distribution?

2.   Discuss the impact of price changes resulting from trade on consumption. What groups will be helped by the trade and what groups will be hurt?

3. Explain how the import restrictions on automobiles, sugar, and clothing in 1984 act as a regressive tax within the U.S. economy.

4. Discuss the potential production and consumption impacts of removing the tariff and quota barriers in the automobile, sugar, and clothing industries.

ANSWERS

True/False Questions
1. True
2. True
3. False
4. False
5. True
6. False
7. False
8. True
9. True
10. False

Fill-in questions
1. autarky
2. autarky equilibrium
3. trade triangle
4. total gains from trade
5. differences in supply conditions; differences in demand conditions

6. differ
7. trade adjustment assistance
8. community indifference curves
9. compensation principle
10. supply conditions

Problems
1.
   a. $(P_x/P_y)_1$
   b. X_1
   c. Y_1
   d. X_1
   e. Y_1
   f. $(P_x/P_y)_2$
   g. E'
   h. X_2
   i. Y_2
   j. C'
   k. X_3
   l. Y_3
   m. E'FC'
   n. CI_1
   o. CI_2

2.
   a. good X
   b. $(P_x/P_y)_1$
   c. E
   d. good Y
   e. $(P_x/P_y)_2$
   f. e
   g. $(P_x/P_y)_3$
   h. E'
   i. x_1
   j. y_1
   k. C'
   l. x_2
   m. y_2
   n. e'
   o. x_3
   p. y_3
   q. c'
   r. x_4
   s. y_4
   t. S_1

73

CHAPTER 7
Offer Curves and the Terms of Trade

SUMMARY

In the previous chapters very little attention has been paid to the price ratio. In this chapter, the determination of international prices will be explored with the use of offer curves. The offer curve indicates the quantity of imports and exports the country is willing to buy and sell on world markets at all possible relative prices. The offer curve is very useful because it combines the demand curve and the supply curve into one curve.

Graphically the offer curves trace out the combinations of exports of one good and imports of the other good the country desires at each possible international price ratio. This is possible because the two axes both measure quantities of the goods. An offer curve diagram can be used to bring both trading countries together in the same graph. The intersection of the two countries' offer curves represents the point at which the quantity of exports country I wishes to sell is exactly equal to the quantity of imports country II wishes to buy AND the quantity of exports country II wishes to sell is exactly equal to the quantity of imports country I wishes to buy. This intersection establishes the equilibrium terms of trade.

In practice, offer curves do not stay fixed. Changes in offer curves occur as countries change their willingness to export or import. An increase in a country's willingness to trade results from an increase in the demand for imports or an increase in the supply of exports. The graphical shift occurs so that each level of imports is now associated with a higher level of exports. An increase in the willingness to trade results in a fall in the terms of trade (the price of the country's export good falls relative to the price of its import good).

A second possibility is a decrease in the country's willingness to trade. This change results from a decrease in the supply of exports or a decrease in the demand for imports. The graphical shift occurs so that each level of imports is associated with a lower level of exports. A decrease in the willingness to trade results in a rise in the terms of trade (the price of the country's export good rises relative to the price of its import good).

As the international terms of trade change inducing movements along an offer curve, the elasticity of the country's demand for imports changes. Graphically the offer curves begin in the elastic range so that a given percentage change in the price of imports will induce a <u>greater</u> percentage change in the quantity of exports purchased. This is the upward sloping portion of the offer curve. When the country moves into the inelastic range of the offer curve, consumers are less sensitive to changes in the import prices. A given percentage change in the price of imports will induce a <u>smaller</u> percentage change in the quantity of imports purchased and the offer curve bends backward. Between these two is the vertical range of the offer curve representing "unit elastic" demand.

The elasticity of offer curves can be crucial in analyzing the impacts of economic growth. Economic growth is assumed to increase a country's willingness to trade leading to a fall in the price of exports relative to imports. The overall impact of this change is dependent on the elasticity of the trading partner's offer curve. If the trading partner is in the elastic range, the decrease in its import prices will result in a relatively large increase in the quantity of imports and overall trade will increase. If the trading partner is in the inelastic range of the offer curve, the decrease in the price of its import good will result in a relatively small change imports. The inelasticity of the partner's offer curve will also cause the fall in the terms of trade to be larger, offsetting some of the benefits of the economic growth.

Elasticity is also crucial when one of the trading countries experiences a change in taste. As a country's taste for imports increases, it is willing to trade more exports for a given amount of imports and experiences a decrease in its terms of trade. The extent of the decrease depends on the elasticity of the trading partner's offer curve. The more inelastic the partner's offer curve the greater the decline in the terms of trade for the country experiencing the taste change.

The offer curve analysis typically compares two economically large countries. A small country is defined in international economies as unable to influence the TOT by its own actions. Graphically, this means that a small country always faces a straight line from the origin representing the international terms of trade. The small country is unable to influence the international TOT no matter where its offer curve is located.

Finally, some distinctions must be made relating to the phrase "terms of trade". The normal use is the price of exports/price of imports or commodity terms of trade. The income terms of trade (the commodity terms of trade multiplied by a quantity index of exports) is used to gauge a nation's export based capacity to buy imports. Attempts to focus on productivity utilize the single factoral terms of trade and the double factoral terms of trade. The choice of measure depends on the trade issue under consideration.

DEFINE THE FOLLOWING KEY TERMS
commodity terms of trade (or net barter terms of trade) (p. 111)

double factoral terms of trade (p. 121)

elasticity of demand for imports (p. 113)

equilibrium terms of trade (p. 106)

income effect (or terms of trade effect) (p. 116)

income terms of trade (p. 120)

large country (p. 118)

offer curve (p. 103)

price index (p. 111)

production effect (p. 116)

single factoral terms of trade (p. 120)

small country (p. 118)

substitution effect (p. 116)

TRUE/FALSE QUESTIONS
1. The offer curve shows the country's willingness to trade with various countries at a particular terms of trade.

2. Offer curves are drawn with quantities measured on both axes rather than price on the vertical axis and quantity on the horizontal axis.

3. At the equilibrium terms of trade, the quantity of exports that country I wishes to sell is exactly equal to the quantity of imports the trading partner wishes to buy.

4. In practice, offer curves are fixed for each country so that the equilibrium terms of trade do not change without government interference.

5. A decrease in a nation's willingness to trade is shown graphically by a shift of an offer curve to represent more of the export good being offered for each quantity of imports.

6. A decline in national income that causes a change in tastes away from the imported good is an example of an increase in a nation's willingness to trade.

7. The upward sloping range of an offer curve is referred to the elastic range of the curve.

8. When a country is located in the inelastic range of the offer curve, a given percentage change in the relative price of imports will induce a larger percentage change in the quantity of imports purchased.

9. When a country experiences economic growth, the decrease in the terms of trade will be larger the more elastic the trading partner's offer curve.

10. If the tastes in a country shift toward a relatively greater preference for the imported good, the change in the terms of trade will be larger the more inelastic the trading partner's offer curve.

FILL-IN QUESTIONS

1. The _____ of a country indicates the quantity of imports and exports a country is willing to buy and sell on world markets at all possible relative prices.

2. The intersection of the offer curves for two countries determines the _____.

3. The price of imports/the price of exports is known as the _____.

4. The percentage change in the quantity of imports demanded divided by the percentage change in the relative price of imports is known as the _____.

5. The _____ effect makes the offer curve upward-sloping because, other things being equal, the higher price the export good is related to a rise in the quantity of exports.

6. The increase in domestic purchases of the export good because of higher real income reduces the amount of the good available for export is an example of the _____ effect.

7. A _____ country is defined in international economics as a country that is unable to influence its terms of trade by its own actions.

8. The commodity terms of trade multiplied by an index of productivity in the export industry is the _____.

9. The commodity terms of trade multiplied by a quantity index of exports is the _____.

10. The single factoral terms of trade divided by the index of productivity in the export industries of trading partners is the _____.

DISCUSSION QUESTIONS
1. Discuss the development of a nation's offer curve using the "trade triangle approach".

2. Graph and explain the determination of the equilibrium terms of trade in a two country case.

3. Graph and explain the impact of an increase in the productivity and supply of exports on the offer curve and terms of trade for a nation.

4. Graph and explain the impact of a decrease in income on the nation's willingness to trade, offer curve, and terms of trade.

5. Explain the relationship between the elasticity of demand for imports and the shape of the offer curve.

6. Discuss the difference between a large country and a small country in terms of the impact of offer curve shifts on the equilibrium terms of trade.

7. Discuss the impact of the elasticity of the trading partner's offer curve on a growing country's terms of trade and volume of trade.

8. Discuss economic situations when the income terms of trade, single factoral terms of trade, and double factoral terms of trade may be more useful than commodity terms of trade.

PROBLEMS

1. Use Figure 3 on page 106 to answer the following questions.

   a. Find the point of trading equilibrium.

   b. Identify the equilibrium terms of trade.

   c. Identify the equilibrium level of exports for country I.

   d. Identify the equilibrium level of exports for country II.

   e. Identify the equilibrium level of imports for country I.

   f. Identify the equilibrium level of imports for country II.

2. Complete the following table of exports and imports at various terms of trade.

Terms of Trade	Quantity Demanded of Imports of Y	Quantity Supplied of Exports of X
1X : 1Y	5 units	(a)
1X : 2Y	18 units	(b)
1X : 3Y	36 units	(c)
1X : 4Y	52 units	(d)

3. Using Figure 5 on page 109, determine the change in country I's offer curve as a result of each change:
   a. an increase in income.

   b. a change in taste away from the imported good.

   c. a increase in productivity in the export industry.

   d. the imposition of a tariff by country I.

CASE STUDY QUESTIONS
Refer to Case Study 1 (p. 112) Terms of Trade for Major Groups of Countries, 1970 - 1995

1. What event had the most profound impact of terms of trade for the period 1970 to 1981. How did this impact show up in Table 2?

2. Some economists argue that developing nations experience a steady decline in their terms of trade relative to developed nations. Does the data in Table 2 support this argument?

3. What group of nations experienced the greatest gain in terms of trade during the study period? What explains this change?

4. What group of nations experienced the greatest decline in terms of trade during the study period? What explains this decline?

Refer to Case Study 2 (p.121) Income Terms of Trade of Major Groups of Countries, 1970 - 1995

1. What is measured by the income terms of trade?

2. What do the increases in the income terms of trade mean for these regional groups?

3. Comparing Tables 2 (p.112) and 3 (p. 121), what regions experienced declines in commodity terms of trade and increases in income terms of trade? How is this possible?

4. What do the increases in the income terms of trade in Table 3 suggest about the volume of trade and welfare of the regions of the world?

ANSWERS

True/False Questions
1. False
2. True
3. True
4. False
5. False
6. False
7. True
8. False
9. False
10. True

Fill-in questions
1. offer curve
2. equilibrium terms of trade
3. commodity terms of trade or net barter terms of trade
4. elasticity of demand for imports
5. substitution
6. income
7. small
8. single factoral terms of trade
9. income terms of trade
10. double factoral terms of trade

Problems
1. a. E
   b. TOT_E
   c. O_xE
   d. O_yE
   e. O_yE
   f. O_xE

2. a. 5 units
   b. 9 units
   c. 12 units
   d. 13 units

3. a. increased willingness to trade (shift to right)
   b. decreased willingness to trade (shift to left)
   c. increased willingness to trade (shift to right)
   d. decreased willingness to trade (shift to left)

CHAPTER 8
The Basis for Trade: Factor Endowments and the Heckscher-Ohlin Model

SUMMARY

Chapter 6 demonstrated the potential gains from trade within the context of the neoclassical model. This chapter also examines potential gains from trade, but places an emphasis on the theoretical model that justifies the trade between nations. The previous examinations concluded that either differences in supply or demand conditions were sufficient to provide a basis for trade. This chapter focuses on the impact of factor availabilities in international trade.

The model is developed under a number of simplifying assumptions. The assumptions are designed to provide two countries that are identical with the exception of their relative endowments of factors. These assumptions result in a two country model in which two homogeneous goods are produced with two homogeneous factors (capital and labor). The nations differ only in their relative endowments of capital and labor.

The differences in the endowments of the two factors mean that the relative abundance of factors will differ. By a physical definition, the ratio of capital to labor will be larger in one nation relative to the other. This higher capital to labor ratio is known as a nation being capital abundant. Relative factor abundance can also be determined by a comparison of relative factor prices. A nation with a relative abundance of capital would be expected to have a price or rental rate of capital (r) that is low relative to the wage rate (w) when compared to the other country. The expectation of a relative abundance of a factor leading to its lower relative price will hold as long as the demand conditions are the same in the two nations.

The production processes associated with each of the two goods is also important to the model. The commodity is said to be labor intensive whenever the ratio of labor to capital used in production is larger than the ratio used to produce the second good. While the substitution of capital for labor is still possible as wage rates increase, the labor intensive commodity will have a higher labor to capital ratio than the other (capital intensive) commodity at all possible factor prices.

The Heckscher-Ohlin (H-O) theorem uses the information on factor abundances and factor intensities to explain the patterns of production and trade. The H-O theorem stated that a country will export the commodity that uses relatively intensively its relatively abundant factor of production, and import the good that uses relatively intensively its relatively scarce factor of production. As a result, a capital abundant country will export the capital intensive good and import the labor intensive good.

The differences in factor endowments contribute to differences in factor prices. A labor abundant country would have relatively low wage rates and relatively high rental rates. This would give the nation a cost advantage in the production of the labor intensive good. Trade with the capital abundant nation will allow the labor abundant nation to import capital intensive goods at a relatively lower price and export labor intensive goods at a relatively higher price. This trade resulting from the new common prices leads to an increase in satisfaction for both nations.

While this is the expected result, Paul Samuelson pointed out that the trade at the new common prices would have an influence on factor prices. As each nation responds to the new prices by increasing the production of their export good, the demand for their abundant factor increase relative to the demand for their scarce factor. In the capital abundant country, increases in the production of the capital intensive product increase the demand for capital relative to labor. This leads to increases in the price of capital relative to wage rates. This result is repeated in reverse for the labor abundant country and is known as the factor price equalization theorem.

Given the results of the factor price equalization theorem, Stolper and Samuelson examined the impact of the trade on income distribution. The Stolper-Samuelson theorem stated that after trade takes place, the increase in the price of the abundant factor and the fall in the price of the scarce factor because of trade imply that the owners of the abundant factor will find their real incomes rising and the owners of the scarce factors will find their incomes falling. The income distribution effect may help explain the tendency of owners of a nation's abundant factors to be more supportive of "free trade" than the owners of the scarce factors.

Some of the assumptions made in the development of the Heckscher-Ohlin theorem are not always applicable in the real world. The following are a few exception to these assumptions that may impact the H-O result. In reality, tastes and preferences are not identical across nations. If a nation's tastes are strongly oriented toward the consumption of the good intensive in its abundant factor, demand reversal may disrupt the H-O outcome. A second problem is related to the factor intensity assumptions. If a product can be capital intensive in one country and labor intensive in another, the problem of factor-intensity reversal exists. Other real world situations that disrupt the H-O outcomes include non-zero transportation costs, imperfect competition, and factors of production that are commodity specific. While these limitations are concerns that must be dealt with, the basic link between relative factor abundance and the pattern of trade remains.

DEFINE THE FOLLOWING KEY TERMS
demand reversal (p. 140)

different factor intensities (p. 128)

different relative factor endowments (p. 128)

factor-intensity reversal (p. 142)

factor price equalization theorem (p. 136)

Heckscher-Ohlin theorem (p. 134)

magnification effect (p. 139)

physical definition of factor abundance (p. 128-129)

price definition of factor abundance (p. 128-129)

specific-factors model (p. 147)

Stolper-Samuelson theorem (p. 138)

TRUE/FALSE QUESTIONS

1. If $(K/L)_I > (K/L)_{II}$, country I would be considered relatively capital abundant by the physical definition of relative factor abundance.

2. Auto production is said to be capital intensive when compared to agriculture if the K/L ratio in auto production is smaller than the K/L ratio in agricultural production.

3. H-O assumes not only that the two commodities have different factor intensities at common factor prices, but also that the difference holds for all possible factor price ratios in both countries.

4. As a result of trade between the two countries, each country will tend to increase the production of the commodity that is intensive in its relatively abundant factor.

5. As product prices converge as a result of trade, the price of the product with the relatively scarce factor increases and the price of the one with the relatively abundant factor falls.

6. In equilibrium, with both countries facing the same relative (and absolute) product prices, both having the same technology with constant returns to scale, relative (and absolute) costs will be equalized.

7. The Stolper-Samuelson theorem suggests that as a result of trade the owners of the abundant factor will find their real income falling and the owners of the scarce factor will find their real incomes rising.

8. In the case of demand reversal, the country is so oriented toward the consumption of the good that intensively uses its relatively abundant factor, that trade will result in falling relative incomes for all consumers.

9. Pure price discrimination by a monopolist leads to the charging of different prices in different markets resulting in higher profits, larger gains from trade, and a greater degree of factor price equalization.

10. While the existence of non-zero transportation costs does not alter the H-O conclusions about the composition of trade, the amount of trade will be reduced.

FILL-IN QUESTIONS

1. If $(r/w)_I > (r/w)_{II}$, country II would be considered relatively _____ abundant by the _____ definition of relative factor abundance.

2. H-O theorem concludes that the country with abundant capital will be able to produce relatively more of the _____-intensive good, while the country with abundant labor will be able to produce relatively more of the _____-intensive good.

3. Assume auto production is capital-intensive while agriculture is labor intensive. If $(r/w)_I < (r/w)_{II}$, H-O theorem would predict that country I will be able to produce _____ relatively more cheaply than country II, and country II will be able to produce _____ relatively more cheaply than country I.

4. H-O predicts that each nation will expand the production and export of the good that made the most intensive use of its relatively _____ factor of production.

5. Trade in final goods essentially substitutes for the movement of factors between countries, leading to a(n) _____ in the price of the abundant factor and a(n) _____ in the price of the scarce factor among participating countries until relative factor prices are _____.

6. The result-that the percentage change in the price of a factor changes more than the percentage change in the price of the good intensive in that factor-is often called the _____ effect.

7. _____ occurs when a commodity has a different factor intensity at different relative prices.

8. A case in which the demand for a country is so oriented toward the good that intensively uses its relatively abundant factor that the relative price of the good is actually higher than the price in the relatively scarce trading partner is referred to as _____.

9. Short run factor immobility between sectors in an H-O context can be examined with a _____ model.

10. Trade based on comparative advantage should tend to increase the demand for the _____ factor and ultimately exert some _____ pressure on its price.

DISCUSSION QUESTIONS
1. Discuss the differences between the physical and the price definitions of relative factor abundance. Under the assumption of identical tastes and preferences, do the two definitions provide different outcomes? Why or why not?

2. Explain the difference between the relative factor abundance of a nation and the relative factor intensity of a commodity.

3. Use the Heckscher-Ohlin theorem to explain the potential gain from trade between nations with different relative factor endowments.

4. Discuss the statement that "trade in final goods essentially substitutes for movement of factors between countries" in terms of factor price equalization.

5. Use the Stolper-Samuelson theorem to explain the division of factor owners between supporters and opponents of free trade.

6. Discuss the potential problems for the Heckscher-Ohlin theorem created by demand reversal and factor intensity reversal.

7. Explain the tendency of non-zero transportation costs to reduce the amount of trade between nations.

8. H-O theory assumes that factors are perfectly mobile between sectors. Discuss the impact of factors that are specific to the production of a particular commodity on the H-O results.

PROBLEMS
1. Assume the following:
   - Banana production is relatively labor intensive
   - Refrigerator production is relatively capital intensive
   - $(K/L)_I < (K/L)_{II}$

   a. Which country is relatively capital abundant?

   b. Which country is relatively labor abundant?

   c. Which country would tend to have a comparative advantage in banana production?

d. Which country would tend to have a comparative advantage in refrigerator production?

2. Given the following information:

Commodity	K/L ($per employee)
grain products	91,000
apparel	16,000
chemicals	132,000
radio and TV equipment	24,000

If the relative factor prices are as follows $(r/w)_I > (r/w)_{II}$ which nation would tend to have the comparative advantage in each of the following commodities:

a. grain products

b. apparel

c. chemicals

d. radio and TV equipment

3. Using Figure 3(b) on page 133, identify the following:
   a. the point of production for country I

   b. the point of production for country II

   c. production of cloth in country I

   d. production of steel in country I

   e. production of cloth in country II

   f. production of steel in country II

g. consumption point for both nations

h. exports by country I

i. imports by country I

j. exports by country II

k. imports by country II

CASE STUDY QUESTIONS
Refer to Case Study 1 (page 129)   Relative Factor Endowments in Selected Countries

1. Which two nations would tend to have the greatest advantage in the production of capital-intensive goods?

2. Which two nations would tend to have the greatest advantage in the production of labor-intensive goods?

3. Discuss the possible interpretations of the relatively high capital/labor ratio in Canada combined with the relatively low capital/land ratio. How can the relatively low capital/labor ratio and relatively high capital/land ratio in Hong Kong be interpreted?

4. What does the labor/land ratio (in column 4) suggest about relative wage rates in the different nations.

Refer to Case Study 2 (page 131)   Relative Factor Intensities in Selected Products

1. What four products would tend to be produced at a lower relative cost in capital abundant nations?

2. What six products would tend to be produced at a lower relative cost in labor abundant nations?

3. Does the information in the case support the H-O assumptions about relative factor intensities? Use 2 commodities to discuss potential gains from trade between two nations.

Refer to Case Study 3 (page 146) The Effect of International Cartels

1. How does the experience of the tungsten market during the 1930s suggest a violation of the H-0 assumption of perfect competition? What was the result?

2. What does the 1939 data on light bulb pricing suggest about price discrimination? How would arbitrage impact this pricing strategy?

3. How does the experience of OPEC in the 1970s differ from the predicted results of the H-O model?

ANSWERS

True/False Questions
1. True
2. False
3. True
4. True
5. False
6. True
7. False
8. False
9. False
10. True

Fill-in Questions
1. capital; price
2. capital; labor
3. autos, agricultural goods
4. abundant
5. increase, fall, equal
6. magnification
7. Factor intensity reversal
8. demand reversal
9. specific factors
10. abundant, upward

Problems
1.   a.   country II
    b.   country I
    c.   country I
    d.   country II

2.   a.   country II
    b.   country I
    c.   country II
    d.   country I

3.   a.   Q
    b.   q
    c. C_2
    d. S_0
    e. C_0
    f. S_2
    g.   C'c'
    h.   country I exports S_0S_1 units of steel
    i.   country I imports C_2C_1 units of cloth
    j.   country II exports C_0C_1 units of cloth
    k.   country II imports S_1S_2 units of steel

CHAPTER 9
Empirical Tests of the Factor Endowments Approach

SUMMARY

The Heckscher-Ohlin model helped to explain why nations have comparative advantages in certain goods. The theorem states that a country will export goods that are relatively intensive in the use of the country's relatively abundant factor. This chapter reviews the attempts to empirically verify the predictions of Heckscher-Ohlin Theorem.

The first major test was conducted by Wassily Leontief in 1953. Leontief used an input-output model to compare the capital to labor ratio of exports and imports. Leontief found that the capital to labor ratio of imports was higher than the capital to labor ratio of exports. These results were in direct contrast to the Heckscher-Ohlin expectation that a capital rich nation like the U.S. would export capital intensive goods and import labor intensive goods. This unexpected outcome became known as the Leontief Paradox.

The Leontief Paradox produced a wide variety of studies attempting to explain the paradox. The resulting explanations include:
   (1) demand reversal
   (2) factor-intensive reversal
   (3) the U.S. tariff bias toward labor intensive goods
   (4) different kinds and qualities of labor
   (5) the need to include natural resources.

While these studies have not eliminated the paradox, they played a major role in reducing the magnitude of the reversal and increasing the understanding of export-import relationships.

The more recent attempts to empirically test the Heckscher-Ohlin theorem have used either a commodity approach or a factor-content approach. The commodity approach relates production characteristics of industries in a country to the net trade position (exports less imports) of the industries. Commodity approach studies have failed to establish a significant link between either physical capital or labor and net exports. The critical factors seem to be human capital and natural resources.

Factor content studies use the Heckscher-Ohlin-Vanek (HOV) theorem which states that the relative factor abundance of a country is revealed through the factor services embodied in the country's trade flows. The results of empirical studies using the HOV model have been very divergent. Leamer (1980) found the U.S. to be capital abundant. Trefler (1993) concluded that the U.S. was abundant in land and scarce in both capital and labor. Maskus (1985) found the U.S. to be abundant in human capital and nonproduction workers. Attempts by Bowen, Leamer, and Sveikauskas (1987) to compare relative factor abundances predicted by HOV analysis with data on actual factor abundances have not been reassuring. The factor-content-version tests may be operating from a theoretical base that is not adequate for interpreting the real world.

While the empirical tests have not provided a glowing endorsement of Heckscher-Ohlin theory, the studies have certainly increased our overall understanding of trade. In particular, there seems to be three elements of interest in a factor endowments approach to trade patterns:
   (1) the factor endowments of a country
   (2) the factor intensity of the production process
   (3) the trade patterns of a country.

Increases in income inequality in the U.S. and Western Europe has been the subject of recent empirical tests. The fact that this rise in inequality has been occurring at the same time that the U.S. and the world have been becoming more open to trade has raised concerns of links to Heckscher-Ohlin and Stolper-Samuelson theorems. The primary focus of the analysis concerns the extent to which rising imports are the <u>cause</u> of the increased income inequality. While the debate continues, current results suggest that trade is a factor in growing income inequality but not a major factor.

DEFINE THE FOLLOWING KEY TERMS

commodity approach or commodity version of Heckscher-Ohlin (p. 162)

factor-content approach or factor-content version of Heckscher-Ohlin (p. 162)

Heckscher-Ohlin-Vanek (HOV) theorem (p. 163)

human capital (p. 162)

input-output table (p. 155)

Leontief paradox (p. 156)

Leontief statistic (p. 156)

multiple regression analysis (p. 162)

total factor requirements (p. 155)

TRUE/FALSE QUESTIONS

1. In an empirical test of the Heckscher-Ohlin theorem, Leontief found that the U.S. exported and imported labor intensive goods thus violating the predictions of the theorem.

2. The Leontief statistic is defined as the capital to labor ratio used in a country to produce imports divided by the capital to labor ratio used to produce exports.

3. According to the Heckscher-Ohlin theorem, the Leontief statistic should be greater than one for a labor abundant country.

4. Demand reversal as an explanation for the Leontief Paradox would require demand patterns across countries to be very similar.

5. In the context of the Leontief Paradox, factor intensity reversal suggests that, although U.S. import goods were produced labor intensively overseas, the production process of these goods in the United States was relatively capital intensive.

6. In the context of the Leontief Paradox, U.S. trade barriers are more concentrated on the imports of relatively capital intensive goods raising the capital to labor ratio of imports relative to U.S. exports.

7. Empirical testing of the Heckscher-Ohlin theorem suggests that the U.S. economy is abundant in physical capital and natural resources and scarce in both skilled and unskilled labor.

8. Rosefielde's 1974 test of the Heckscher-Ohlin theorem in the Soviet Union suggested that the Soviet Union was capital abundant when compared to its Eastern European trading partners but labor abundant when compared to Western Europe and the United States.

9. The commodity approach to testing the Heckscher-Ohlin theorem by Stern and Maskus (1981) indicates that net exports are positively correlated with the amount of human capital.

10. The results of the empirical testing of the Heckscher-Ohlin suggest that the theorem has absolutely no relevance in the real world of international trade.

FILL-IN QUESTIONS

1. An empirical test of the Heckscher-Ohlin theorem by the commodity approach results in the following findings:

    (X-M) = -14.68 + 0.09K + 0.14H - 2.06L.

    These results suggest that physical capital is _____ related to net exports, human capital is _____ related to net exports, and labor is _____ related to net exports.

2. Trefler's (1993) analysis of the Heckscher-Ohlin theorem suggests that in 1983 the U.S. economy was relatively abundant in _____ and relatively scarce in both _____ and _____.

3. According to the H-O theorem, a relatively capital abundant country would have a Leontief statistic with a value of _____ while a relatively labor abundant country would have a Leontief statistic with a value _____.

4. A Leontief statistic of 1.44 for Mexico would suggest that Mexico is a relatively _____-abundant country.

5. The belief that demand patterns across trading partners differ to such an extent that trade does not follow the H-O pattern is an explanation known as _____.

6. In an attempt to explain the Leontief paradox some suggest that U.S. tariffs concentrated on _____ goods result in a bundle of imports that is more capital-intensive than would be the case in the absence of barriers.

7. The belief that the Leontief Paradox occurs because some goods are produced by relatively capital-intensive methods in one country but are produced by relatively labor-intensive methods in other countries is known as _____.

8. Stolper and Roskamp's analysis of 1961 trade patterns of the German Democratic Republic (GDR) suggested that the GDR was exporting _____-intensive goods and importing _____-intensive goods in their trade with other Eastern European Nations.

9. Using H-O-V analysis, Maskus (1985) reported that in factor abundance rankings for the U.S. economy in 1958 _____ were most abundant while _____ was least abundant.

10. Deardorff (1994) pointed out that the <u>three</u> elements of interest in the Heckscher-Ohlin factor endowments approach to trade are:

    (1) _____
    (2) _____
    (3) _____.

DISCUSSION QUESTIONS

1. Discuss the empirical analysis that led to the Leontief Paradox. How do demand reversal and factor-intensity reversal help to explain the paradox?

2. Many economists suggest that using capital and labor as the only two factors in the H-O analysis may be a potential problem. Discuss the results of considering different skill levels of labor and natural resources in the empirical analysis of the H-O theorem.

3. Assume U.S. tariffs on the import of relatively labor-intensive goods contribute to the Leontief Paradox. Explain the expected impact of a free trade agreement on the Leontief statistic and the Leontief paradox.

4. Maskus, using H-O-V analysis, found engineers and scientists to be the factor most abundant in the net export of factor services by the U.S. in 1958 and 1972. If you were to repeat this analysis using current data, would you expect to find the same results? Why or why not?

5. Using a commodity approach to testing H-O theorem, set up a multiple regression model to analyze U.S. net exports and explain the variables you included in the model. Discuss the expected correlation between each variable and net exports.

6. Discuss the potential link between the Heckscher-Ohlin and Stolper-Samuelson theorems and the growing income inequality in the U.S. and Western Europe.

7. Using the work of Adrian Wood, build a case for increased trade with developing nations as a cause for increased income inequality in developed countries.

8. Discuss the role of factors other than trade in the rising income inequality in developed nations.

PROBLEMS

1. Assume that exports utilize $3.4 million worth of capital and 170 years of labor time and imports utilize $5.1 million worth of capital and 300 years of labor time.

    a. Calculate the Leontief statistic.

    b. Given your result in **a.** would you expect this nation to be capital abundant or labor abundant?

2. The following are results from a multiple regression analysis
    $(X - M) = -20.67 + 0.26K + 0.11H - 2.03L$
    where X stands for exports of a product, M stands for imports, K represents physical capital, H represents human capital, and L represents the level of industry employment.

    a. Net exports are positively related to which factors in the model.

    b. Net exports are negatively related to which factors in the model.

    c. Discuss the impact of the addition of $1 worth of physical capital in an industry on net exports.

d. Discuss the impact of the addition of $1 worth of human capital in an industry on net exports.

e. Discuss the impact of the addition of one more unit of employment to an industry on net exports.

3. Assume the ten industries listed have on average the following capital/labor ratios:

Industry	K/L
Wholesale trade	$ 7,500
Motor vehicles	$12,200
Agriculture and fisheries	$20,750
Rubber	$ 8,200
Food Products	$ 6,400
Furs	$11,400
Coal Mining	$ 9,875
Steel Works	$22,150
Pulp Mill Products	$14,600
Textile Mill Products	$19,350

a. According to Heckscher-Ohlin theorem, a capital-abundant country would be most likely to export which five products?

b. According to Heckscher-Ohlin theorem, a labor-abundant country would be most likely to export which five products?

c. List 3 possible explanations for the case in which a capital-abundant country exports Food Products and imports Steel.

CASE STUDY QUESTIONS
Refer to Case Study 1 (p.157) Capital/Labor Ratios in Leading Export and Import Industries, Leontief Test

1. Using the information from Table 1, identify industries that supported the Leontief Paradox (capital/labor ratio of net importers exceeds net exporters).

2. Using the industries in Table 1, revise the capital/labor ratios so that the Leontief Paradox disappears. Use these new capital/labor ratios to revise Figure 1.

3. Discuss the potential impact of the U.S. tariff structure on the Leontief paradox.

4. In many cases, industries that were net exporters in 1947 are now net importers. What changes in the economy could help to explain this shift in comparative advantage over time?

Refer to Case Study 2 (p.157) Factor Content of Trade, Selected Countries

1. Given the information in Table 2, identify the nation(s) with a revealed abundance in each of the following factors:
   a. capital stock

   b. total labor force

   c. managerial workers

   d. service workers

   e. arable land

2. If the production of a particular good is intensive in the use of capital and arable land, what nation would you expect to have a comparative advantage?

3. If the production of a particular good is intensive in agricultural workers and pasture land, what nation would you expect to have a comparative advantage?

4. If the production of a particular good is intensive in professional/technical workers, managerial workers, and production workers, what nations would you expect to have comparative advantages?

5. Discuss any changes in revealed factor abundance that may have occurred from 1967 to the present.

ANSWERS

True/False Questions
1. False
2. True
3. True
4. False
5. True
6. False
7. False
8. True
9. True
10. False

Fill-in questions
1. positively; positively; negatively
2. land; capital; labor
3. less than 1.0; greater than 1.0
4. labor
5. demand reversal
6. labor intensive
7. factor intensity reversal
8. capital; labor
9. engineers and scientists; physical capital
10. factor endowments of the country
    factor intensities of the production processes
    trade pattern of the country

Problems
1.   a.   (5.1/300)/(3.4/170) = 17/20
    b.   the Leontief statistic is less than 1 so the country would be relatively capital-abundant

2.   a.   physical capital and human capital
    b.   level of industry employment
    c.   the addition of $1 worth of physical capital will result in $0.26 more net exports
    d.   the addition of $1 worth of human capital will result in $0.11 more net exports
    e.   the addition of one more unit of employment will reduce net exports by $2.03.

3.   a.   Motor Vehicles
          Agriculture and Fisheries
          Steel Works
          Pulp Mill Products
          Textile Mill Products

    b.   Wholesale trade
          Rubber
          Food Products
          Furs
          Coal Mining

    c.   Any three from this list: Demand reversal, Factor-intensity reversal, tariff structure, labor skills, natural resources

CHAPTER 10
Post-Heckscher-Ohlin Theories of Trade and Intra-Industry Trade

SUMMARY
Empirical testing of the Heckscher-Ohlin theorem raised questions about the restrictive assumptions and results of the model. This chapter examines some more recent attempts to relax the H-O assumptions and explain the causes and consequences of trade. An early attempt was seen in the imitation lag hypothesis. This hypothesis focuses on differences in technology availability and demand between countries. The model suggests that when a new product is developed in one country there will be a lag before it is demanded by consumers in other countries. Once the demand arises, the nations must import the product from the originating nation until they develop the technology necessary to produce the product.

The imitation lag hypothesis was expanded to form the product cycle theory. The theory focuses on the development of a new manufactured product in a research oriented country. During the first stage, the new product stage, the product is produced and consumed only in the nation of origin. In the second stage, the maturing product stage, production becomes more standardized and the product is exported to other nations. The exports may be followed by production in other developed nations. The final stage, the standardized product stage, is marked by the product and the production process being well known worldwide. In the final stage, production shifts to developing countries and the originating nation becomes an importer. The developed countries are busy developing new products. These models provide a better explanation of dynamic comparative advantages. Markusen et al. (1995) suggest that there is a similar cycle for techniques of production and machinery.

A third alternative departs from the H-O theorem by focusing on demand. The Linder theory hypothesizes that consumer tastes are conditioned by income levels and that the goods produced by a country will be a reflection of the nation's income level. The result is that international trade will be more intense between countries with similar income levels. With product differentiation, a country may be importing and exporting goods from the same product classification.

The Kemp model examines the impact of increasing returns to scale in production of both commodities in a two good model. The results of considering increasing returns to scale include a convex production possibility frontier and unstable equilibria. The relaxation of the constant returns to scale assumption calls into question some of the certainty of the conclusions of traditional trade theory.

The Krugman model makes two major adjustments to traditional trade models by allowing increasing returns to scale and monopolistic competition. The removal of perfect competition allows differentiated products and a downward sloping demand curve for each product. Krugman examines two identical nations and finds (contrary to the H-O outcome) that gains from trade are possible. The larger combined markets allow gains from economies of scale and consumers gain from obtaining similar but differentiated goods. Krugman demonstrates increases in real wages and output in both countries reinforcing the gains possible from trade.

Krugman has also examined the geographic component of location of production. Once production begins in a region, cost advantages related to economies of scale, pooling of labor, and availability of specialized inputs may result in a concentration of production and regional/international comparative advantage. Once established, this regional production generates a dynamics of its own and tends to be self-sustaining.

Many of the new trade theories recognize the importance of intra-industry trade (importing and exporting goods from the same product classification). Some of the possible explanations for intra-industry trade include:
- (1) product differentiation
- (2) transportation costs and geographic location
- (3) dynamic economies of scale
- (4) degree of product aggregation
- (5) differing income distributions.

Empirical analysis has revealed that greater per capita income, greater national income, greater openness, and a common border are positively correlated with the extent of intra-industry trade.

DEFINE THE FOLLOWING KEY TERMS
demand lag (p. 175)

dynamic comparative advantage (p. 177)

dynamic economies of scale (p. 195)

imitation lag (p. 175)

imitation lag hypothesis (p. 175)

inter-industry trade (p. 194)

intra-industry trade (p. 194)

Kemp model (p. 184)

Krugman model (p. 187)

Linder theory (p. 180)

maturing product stage (p. 176)

monopolistic competition (p. 187)

net lag (p. 176)

new product stage (p. 176)

overlapping demand (p. 181)

product cycle theory (p. 176)

product differentiation (p. 184)

standardized product stage (p. 177)

technology cycle (p. 180)

TRUE/FALSE QUESTIONS
1. In the imitation lag hypothesis, the demand lag refers to the length of time between the consumers' demand for an import and the arrival of the imported good.

2. The product cycle theory examines three stages in the life cycle of a good originated in a developing nation and imported by more developed nations like the U.S.

3. The second stage of the product cycle theory is known as the maturing product stage.

4. The Linder theory is a dramatic departure from the H-O model because it focuses almost exclusively on factor endowments.

5. The fact that two different brands of automobiles are not the same in a consumer's mind is an example of product differentiation.

6. The Kemp model added substantial support for the certainty of outcomes in the H-O model by allowing increasing returns to scale in both industries.

7. The existence of increasing returns to scale in both industries in the Kemp model results in a concave production possibility frontier.

8. The Krugman model examines two countries that are identical in all respects and concludes that these two countries have no reason to trade.

9. Intra-industry trade occurs when a country is both exporting and importing items in the same product classification category.

10. The possible explanations for the occurrence of intra-industry trade include product differentiation, geographical location, and differences in income distribution.

FILL-IN QUESTIONS
1. The length of time that elapses between a products introduction in the first country and the appearance of a version of the product in a second country is known as the _____.

2. The first stage of the product cycle theory is known as the _____.

3. The stage of the product cycle theory in which the product and production process are well known and production begins in developing nations is known as the _____ stage.

4. A trade model that is a dramatic departure from the Heckscher-Ohlin model because it adds economies of scale and monopolistic competition is the _____ model.

5. An exclusively demand oriented trade theory that focuses on the relationship between income levels and goods produced is known as the _____ theory.

6. A trade model that assumes increasing returns to scale and a convex PPF resulting in an unstable autarky equilibrium is known as the _____ model.

7. Advertising and sales promotions by firms attempting to differentiate their products in the minds of consumers occurs in the market structure known as _____.

8. When a country is both exporting and importing items in the same product classification category it is known as _____.

9. _____ trade occurs when a country's exports and imports are in different product classification categories.

10. Per-unit cost reductions that occur because of experience in producing a particular good are known as _____.

DISCUSSION QUESTIONS
1. Choose a particular manufactured product that fits the product cycle theory and discuss its development through all three stages.

2. In Chapter 1, an examination of trade patterns suggests that the majority of trade occurs between developed nations. Use the Linder theory to explain this trade pattern. What does the theory suggest about trade between developed and developing nations?

3. Traditional trade models suggest that nations with identical tastes and resource endowments have no basis for trade. Discuss the major ways that the results of Krugman's model differ from the traditional results.

4. Empirical results have suggested that the extent of intra-industry trade is positively related to greater per capita income, greater national income, greater openness, and common borders. Use these results to discuss the fact that Canada is the U.S.'s largest trading partner.

5. Discuss the impact of economies of scale on specialization in the Kemp model. How is opening a nation to trade in the Krugman model related to economies of scale?

6. Krugman discussed the role of geography in trade. List the factors that may lead to a concentration of production in a particular region. How can government policies influence this process?

PROBLEMS
1. Assume the imitation lag for a new product is 12 months and the demand lag is 3 months.
   a. Determine the net lag for the new product.

   b. Will trade occur in the product during the first two months after the introduction of the product? Why or why not.

   c. Discuss the pattern of trade after the demand lag is over.

2. A new computer is developed by a U.S. manufacturer. Given the following values of U.S. imports and exports of the computers, determine the corresponding stage of the product cycle theory.

   a. exports = $1.5 billion; imports = 0

   b. exports = 0; imports = 0

   c. exports = 0; imports = $1.28 billion

3. In the Krugman model, the labor equation for the monopolistically competitive firm is:
   $$L_i = 5 + 3Q_i.$$

   a. Determine the labor input necessary to produce 10 units of output.

   b. Determine the labor input necessary to produce 20 units of output.

   c. Is this firm experiencing increasing, constant, or decreasing returns to scale?

4. Given the following relationship between price and marginal revenue:
$$P = MR [e_D/(e_D + 1)].$$

   a. If MR = $10 and $e_D = -3$, find the price of output.

   b. If MR remains $10 but $e_D = -2$, find the price of output.

   c. As the elasticity of demand changes from -3 to -2, demand for the good becomes more/less elastic and the resulting price rises/falls.

CASE STUDY QUESTIONS
Refer to Case Study 1 (p.179) Product Age and Industry Characteristics

1. In analyzing Table 1, discuss the expected results for exports and imports as a percentage of industry sales to support the product cycle theory.

2. Why would R & D and marketing expenses as a percentage of revenue be valuable in verifying the existence of the product cycle theory?

3. Discuss the expected pattern of real market growth through the 3 stages of product cycle theory.

4. If you were attempting to update Thorelli and Burnett's analysis, what changes would you suggest? What types of products would you use for your sample?

Refer to Case Study 2 (p.182) Demand Patterns across Countries

1. Given Linder's assumption that consumption patterns are determined by income levels and that a nation's production is related to its consumption patterns, determine which categories of goods would receive the greatest concentration of productive resources in:

   a. high income economies

   b. upper middle income economies

   c. lower middle income economies

   d. low income economies.

2. Given the consumption patterns in Table 2, discuss the problems experienced by low income economies as they attempt to increase their exports to high income economies.

3. Using these categories of economies, explain the progression of a new product through the 3 stages of the product cycle theory.

4. Use the concept of overlapping demand to determine potential trade patterns between the members of the 4 income categories.

Refer to Case Study 3 (p. 188) Product Differentiation in the U.S. Automobile Industry

1. Explain the role of product differentiation in the extensive intra-industry trade in automobiles.

2. Discuss the impact of Japanese auto manufacturers opening U.S. production facilities on intra-industry trade in auto parts.

3. Discuss the impact of differences in income distribution on the degree of product differentiation and intra-industry trade in the U.S. auto market.

4. What do the number of cars exported and imported indicate about the stage the U.S. is in on the product cycle?

5. Given the following cars from Table 3, what would Linder's theory suggest about the nations importing these vehicles?

        Lincoln Town Car

        Geo Metro

        Cadillac DeVille

        Ford Escort

ANSWERS

True/False Questions
1. False
2. False
3. True
4. False
5. True
6. False
7. False
8. False
9. True
10. True

Fill-in questions
1. imitation lag
2. new product stage
3. standardized product
4. Krugman
5. Linder
6. Kemp
7. monopolistic competition
8. intra-industry trade
9. inter-industry
10. dynamic economies of scale

Problems
1. a. 12 - 3 = 9 months
   b. no trade because with 3 months of demand lag, consumers in the importing nation will not demand the product in the first two months.
   c. during months 4 - 12 the originating nation will export the product to the second nation. After 12 months, production will take place in the second nation.

2. a. stage 2 maturing product stage
   b. stage 1 new product stage
   c. stage 3 standardized product stage

3. a. $L_i = 5 + 3(10) = 35$
   b. $L_i = 5 + 3(20) = 65$
   c. increasing returns to scale

4. a. $P = 10(-3/-3 + 1) = 10(3/2) = 15$
   b. $P = 10(-2/-2 + 1) = 10(2) = 20$
   c. less; rises

CHAPTER 11
Economic Growth and International Trade

SUMMARY
To this point, most of the analysis has assumed that the production possibility frontier of a country remains fixed. In practice, a nation's PPF is continually changing. This chapter focuses on growth in output potential from changes in technology and the acquisition of additional resources.

Economic growth has an impact on both producers and consumers. The classification of these impacts will discussed under the assumption of a small country. As the production possibility frontier shifts outward the changes in production fall into three basic categories. The first is the production of more of both commodities in the same proportion as before the growth - a neutral trade production effect. The second possibility is to increase the production of both goods but relatively more of one than the other. If relatively more of the export good is produced this is a protrade production effect. If relatively more of the import-competing good is produced the result is an antitrade production effect. The final possibility is the increase in the production of one good so much that the production of the other good decreases. If the increase in production is in the export good, this is classified as an ultra-protrade production effect. If the increase in production is in the import-competing good the result is classified as an ultra-antitrade production effect.

Economic growth has an impact on consumption as well. Changes in consumption are classified in a manner very similar to production growth. If the relative consumption of the two goods remains the same, the growth reflects a neutral-trade consumption effect. If the consumption of both goods increase but the proportions change there are two possible classifications. If the relatively larger increase is in the imported good, the change is a protrade consumption effect. If the relatively larger change in consumption is in the export good, the change is an antitrade consumption effect. Finally, if the growth results in an increase in the consumption so large that the consumption of the second good declines, the effects are classified as ultra-protrade or ultra-antitrade according to the good experiencing the increase in consumption. The net result of changes in production and consumption on a country's trade can be determined by examining the country's income elasticity of demand for imports.

The actual growth may be the result of technological growth or greater accumulation of factors. The technological changes can be factor neutral, labor saving, or capital saving. Factor growth may also have differential effects. Equal growth in both factors will have a neutral impact on growth. A growth in capital only will have a relatively larger impact on the production of capital-intensive goods. Growth in the labor force only, will have a relatively larger impact on labor-intensive products. The cases of non-neutral growth will shift the PPF in an asymmetrical manner.

For a small country, an increase in one factor only will result in an increase in the production of the good intensive in that factor and a decrease in the production of the other good.

In other words, the production effect will either be ultra-protrade or ultra-antitrade. This conclusion is known as the Rybczynski theorem. The welfare effects of the factor growth or technological changes will all be positive in the small country case with the exception of population growth.

The large country case becomes a bit more complicated. Changes in production or consumption by a large country may have an impact on the international price of the goods shifting the offer curve. This means that economic growth may have effects on the terms of trade. The worst case would have the negative terms of trade effects outweigh the positive growth effects. This is known as immiserizing growth.

For developing countries, there are some special considerations. When the nations are major producers of an export, adverse terms of trade movements may reduce the benefits of growth. Differences in the income elasticity of demand for imports may lead to an ultra-protrade consumption effect and balance-of-trade deficits.

DEFINE THE FOLLOWING KEY TERMS
antitrade consumption effect (p. 205)

antitrade production effect (p. 205)

capital-saving technological change (p. 207)

commodity-neutral technological change (p. 208)

endogenous growth models (p. 208)

factor-neutral growth effect (p. 210)

factor-neutral technological change (p. 207)

immiserizing growth (p. 217)

income elasticity of demand for imports (p. 206)

labor-saving technological change (p. 207)

neutral-trade consumption effect (p. 205)

neutral-trade production effect (p. 204-205)

protrade consumption effect (p. 205)

protrade production effect (p. 205)

Rybczynski theorem (p. 213)

ultra-antitrade consumption effect (p. 205)

ultra-antitrade production effect (p. 205)

ultra-protrade consumption effect (p. 205)

ultra-protrade production effect (p. 205)

TRUE/FALSE QUESTIONS

1. Economic growth comes about by means of a change in technology or through the acquisition of additional resources such as labor, capital or human capital.

2. An Ultra-protrade production effect would suggest an increase in the production of the export good and a decrease in the production of the import-competing good.

3. An ultra-protrade consumption effect would suggest an increase in the consumption of the export good and a decrease in the consumption of the imported good.

4. A technological change that decreases the capital to labor ratio (K/L) would be considered labor saving.

5. If a nation's capital stock increases but the size of the labor force remains constant, the PPF cannot shift outward because there are no workers to utilize the new capital.

6. A PPF that shifts out asymmetrically in the direction of the labor intensive good would suggest an increase in labor without a corresponding increase in the capital stock.

7. Economic growth that leads to ultra-antitrade consumption and production effects actually causes trade to decline.

8. The Rybczynski theorem concludes that growth in one factor leads to an expansion of the production of both goods but the increase will be relatively larger for the good intensive in the growing factor.

9. For growth to be beneficial in the large trading country, the negative terms of trade effects must not completely offset the positive effects of growth.

10. Technological advances in developing countries combine with relatively low wages to decrease the costs of production of manufactured goods relative to primary products leading to terms of trade improvements in the long run.

FILL-IN QUESTIONS

1. New production points that represent increases in the production of both goods with a relatively larger increase in the import-competing good is known as a _____ production effect.

2. New production points that represent increases in the production of both goods in the same proportion is known as a _____ production effect.

3. New consumption that represents increased consumption of both goods with a relatively larger increase in the imported good is known as a _____ consumption effect.

4. New consumption that represents an increased consumption of the export good and a decreased consumption of the import good is known as an _____ consumption effect.

5. The measure of the percentage change in imports divided by the percentage change in national income is the _____,

6. A new technology that results in the same relative amounts of capital and labor being used as before the technology changed would be _____.

7. A _____ saving technological change has an impact equivalent to increasing the relative amount of labor available to the economy.

8. In the small country case, an increase in population will lead to a _____ in per capita income, other things being equal.

9. In the large country case, the situation where the negative terms of trade effects outweigh the positive growth effects is referred to as _____.

10. Primary goods tend to have income elasticities _____ than 1.0, while manufactures tend to be characterized by an income elasticity _____ than 1.0.

DISCUSSION QUESTIONS

1. Assume Mexico is a small country that cannot influence world prices. Mexico exports textiles and imports automobiles. Discuss the five different production effects from economic growth in terms of change in the production of textiles and automobiles.

    a

    b.

    c.

    d.

    e.

2. Assume that Mexico is a small country from the standpoint of consumption also. Discuss the five different consumption effects from economic growth in terms of changes in the consumption of textiles and automobiles.

3. Discuss the ultimate impact of economic growth on trade in the following situations:
   a. Ultra-antitrade consumption and production effects
   b. neutral-trade consumption and production effects
   c. protrade consumption effect and ultra-protrade production effect

4. Discuss the relationships between trade growth and income growth under the following income elasticity of import demand (YEM) conditions:

   a. YEM = 1.0

   b. YEM > 1.0

   c. 0 < YEM < 1

   d. YEM < 0

5. In the case of a country with two homogeneous inputs, capital and labor, discuss the impact on growth of an increase in the capital stock only, an increase in the labor force only, and an equivalent increase in both.

6. Discuss the impact of an increase only in a country's labor force when the labor-intensive good is a country's export good. How does your answer change if the labor-intensive good is the nation's import good? Frame these answers in terms of the Rybczynski theorem and the small country assumption.

7. Discuss the additional concerns that arise when the nation experiencing economic growth is assumed to be a large country.

8. Discuss the special concerns associated with the impacts of adverse terms-of-trade movements in the case of developing countries. How are these effects related to price and income elasticity issues?

PROBLEMS

1. Using Figure 1(b) on page 204, classify the production effect of the following production points:
   a. a point on the new PPF in region IV.

   b. a point on the new PPF in region II.

   c. a point on the new PPF in region III.

   d. a point on the new PPF in region I.

   e. a point on the new PPF along the ray from the origin through Point A.

2. Using Figure 2 on page 206, classify the consumption effect of the following consumption points:
   a. a new consumption point on the ray from the origin through B.

   b. a new consumption point in region I.

   c. a new consumption point in region II.

   d. a new consumption point in region III.

   e. a new consumption point in region IV.

CASE STUDY QUESTIONS
Refer to Case Study 1 (p. 208) Labor and Capital Requirements per Unit of Output

1. Using the information in figure 4, rank the changes in the capital to labor ratio (K/L) in these six countries between 1964 and 1985.

2. Use the relative changes in capital and labor usage to discuss differences in the level of economic development and productivity growth between these nations.

3. In 1985, which nations are using the more capital intensive production methods? What does this suggest about the relative costs of capital and labor in these countries?

Refer to Case Study 2 (p. 221) Terms of Trade of Kenya, South Korea, Pakistan, and Venezuela, 1980-1995

1. Using the information in figure 15, determine which nation experienced the largest decrease in terms of trade and which nation experienced the largest increase in terms of trade.

2. A press release suggests that changes in terms of trade are positively related to economic growth. Using the countries in this case, prepare your response to this statement.

3. A movement from dependence on primary products to greater diversification in production is often suggested as a means to reduce terms of trade instability. Do the nations in this case lend support for this view? Why or why not?

ANSWERS

True/False Questions
1. True
2. True
3. False
4. False
5. False
6. True
7. True
8. False
9. True
10. False

Fill-in Questions
1. antitrade
2. neutral-trade
3. protrade
4. ultra-antitrade
5. income elasticity of demand for imports
6. factor neutral
7. labor
8. fall
9. immiserizing growth
10. less, greater

Problems
1.
   a. ultra-antitrade production effect
   b. ultra-protrade production effect
   c. antitrade production effect
   d. protrade production effect
   e. neutral-trade production effect

2.
   a. neutral-trade consumption effect
   b. antitrade consumption effect
   c. ultra-antitrade consumption effect
   d. protrade consumption effect
   e. ultra-protrade consumption effect

CHAPTER 12
International Factor Movements

SUMMARY

In the early chapters, it was assumed that factors of production could not move from one country to another. This chapter relaxes those assumptions and focuses on international movements of capital and labor. Capital movements between nations can be through foreign direct investment and foreign portfolio investment.

Foreign direct investment involves ownership and control. When a foreign firm purchases more than 50 percent of the company, it becomes a foreign subsidiary. Foreign direct investment is normally discussed in the context of a multinational corporation (MNC). MNCs have production taking place in branch plants in two or more countries with supervision and control based in one country. The flow of financial capital to another country without ownership or control is referred to as foreign portfolio investment.

Direct Foreign Investment has exhibited substantial growth since 1960. The U.S. is the source of more DFI than any other nation and a major recipient. Europe and Canada are the primary recipients of U.S. investments. The major reason for capital movements between nations is the expectation of a higher rate of return in the new location. Additional hypotheses to explain the movement include:
(1) locating plants in growing markets
(2) manufacturing and service production catering to high income tastes and wants
(3) securing access to minerals and raw materials
(4) avoiding tariff and non-tariff barriers
(5) seeking low relative wages
(6) investing to protect the share of a foreign market
(7) diversifying risk
(8) exploit a particular advantage in another market.

Analytically, differences in the marginal productivity of capital between two nations is the basis of capital mobility. As capital moves from one nation to another, the marginal productivities equalize and world output and efficiency are increased. The impact of the factor movement on factor price equalization leads economists to discuss free trade and free factor mobility as substitutes. In practice, the movement of capital entails both costs and benefits.

Potential gains include increased output, wages, employment, exports, and tax revenues. Additionally, there is the potential for the realization of scale economies, development of technical and managerial skills, and weakening the power of domestic monopolies. The direct foreign investment may also result in certain costs. The capital inflow may have an adverse impact on the host country's terms of trade, saving rate, domestic investment, and unemployment. Other concerns involve the sovereignty of the host country, inadequate development of skills, monopolization of industries, balance of payment instability, and the pricing behavior of MNCs.

International factor movements can also involve labor. There are a variety of potential reasons for this migration, but differences in wage levels is critical. Analytically, the movement of homogeneous labor from one nation to another should result in wage equalization. In practice, this equalization has not occurred. Differences in skill levels, the temporary status of immigrants, immigration policies, language and cultural barriers all interfere with the equalization of wages.

The type of worker moving from one country to another has an impact on the analysis of costs and benefits of the movement. Unskilled workers tend to suffer greater employment instability and are generally linked with higher social maintenance costs. The movement of skilled workers can increase productivity and result in positive externalities for the recipient nation with little or no indirect social cost. This brain drain can seriously decrease the skill level of the source country's labor force and prevent the realization of the benefits of substantial human capital investments. Developing nations are attempting to develop policies to control brain drain.

International factor movements in the form of immigration into the U.S. have been the subject of a large volume of recent research. The results of this research suggest that the economic characteristics of the immigrants have been changing. A larger relative share are coming from developing countries and there has been a decline in the relative skill levels. The concern is that the declining skill level may have contributed to the relative decline in wages in the 1980s.

DEFINE THE FOLLOWING KEY TERMS
brain drain (p. 243)

branch plant (p. 226)

foreign direct investment (p. 225)

foreign portfolio investment (p. 225)

foreign subsidiary (p. 226)

guest worker (p. 241)

host countries (p. 227)

multinational corporation (MNC) or multinational enterprise (MNE) or transnational corporation (TNC) or transnational enterprise (TNE) (p. 226)

performance requirements (p. 236)

surplus labor (p. 238)

tariff factories (p. 229)

transfer pricing (p. 234)

TRUE/FALSE QUESTIONS
1. The movement of capital from one nation to another that involves ownership and control is known as foreign portfolio investment.

2. A U.S. firm with plants in three different states that exports to 27 nations is considered to be a multinational corporation (MNC).

3. The largest recipient of U.S. FDI is the United Kingdom while Japan is the largest source of FDI into the U.S.

4. Japan is home to the world's largest corporation and the world's largest bank.

5. High tariff and non-tariff barriers may actually lead to an increase in FDI within the nation.

6. Direct investment in a country may be to secure access to a raw material or to employ relatively low priced labor.

7. The potential benefits of FDI include increased capital imports and increased unemployment.

8. FDI may actually lead to decreases in the rates of domestic saving and domestic investment.

9. Guest worker programs often allow low-skilled workers to immigrate for short periods of time and can require the workers to leave at the government's request.

10. Policies designed to prevent brain drain include highly progressive tax rates and income ceilings.

FILL-IN QUESTIONS

1. If a U.S. multinational corporation builds and controls a plant in Mexico the Mexican facility is known as a _____.

2. If a U.S. firm purchases more than 50 percent of the outstanding stock in a Mexican plant, the Mexican firm becomes a _____.

3. _____ is the region that is the largest recipient of U.S. foreign direct investment.

4. Firms may invest in foreign production facilities for defensive purposes in order to protect _____.

5. If the foreign investor is able to take advantage of market size and technological features in order to realize economies of scale, consumer price in the host country might be _____.

6. The MNC's arbitrary recording of the price of intrafirm trade to help maximize profits and minimize taxes is known as _____.

7. In an attempt to obtain the benefits of FDI while minimizing the costs, _____ are frequently placed on the foreign firms.

8. Assuming labor is homogeneous in two countries, labor should move from areas of _____ and _____ wages to areas of _____ and _____ wages.

9. A nation with an excess supply of labor is said to possess _____ labor.

10. The movement of highly educated workers from developing nations to developed nations is known as the _____.

DISCUSSION QUESTIONS

1. While capital moves from one nation to another in search of higher returns, discuss the alternative hypotheses associated with this flow of capital resources.

2. Free trade and freedom of factor movements are said to be substitutes. Discuss the concept of factor price equalization in terms of the movement of productive factors.

3. Outline the costs and benefits of foreign direct investment from the perspective of the host country.

4. Discuss the impact of two different skill levels on the wages paid and output in a nation receiving immigrant workers.

5. Describe the cost associated with the brain drain from developing countries and some of the policies designed to prevent these losses.

6. Discuss the potential impacts of cross-cultural differences on labor migration and foreign direct investment.

PROBLEMS

1. Using Table 1 (p. 226) identify the following:
   a. the region that is the recipient of the greatest amount of U.S. foreign direct investment.

   b. the two industries in which most of the foreign direct investment is concentrated.

   Using Table 2 (p. 227) identify the following:
   c. the region responsible for the most foreign direct investment in the U.S.

   d. the two industries that are the recipient of the majority of direct foreign investment in the U.S.

2. Refer to Figure 1 (p. 232) to answer the following questions about capital movements in a two country world.
   a. What is the initial capital stock in country I?

   b. What is the initial capital stock in country II?

   c. What is the total world capital stock?

   d. What is the initial rental rate for capital in country I?

   e. What is the initial rental rate for capital in country II?

   f. If capital is allowed to move freely from one country to the other, what is the direction of the flow?

g. What happens to the rate of return on capital in country I?

h. What happens to the rate of return on capital in country II?

i. What is the new capital allocation for each country?

j. What change occurs in country I's output?

k. What changes occur in country II's output?

l. What changes occur in world output?

3. Refer to Figure 2 (p. 238) to answer the following questions about labor movements in a two-country world with homogeneous labor.
   a. What is the total supply of labor available in both countries?

   b. What is the initial supply of labor in country I?

   c. What is the initial supply of labor in country II?

   d. What is the initial wage rate in country I?

   e. What is the initial wage rate in country II?

f. If labor is allowed to move from one country to the other, what will the new equilibrium wage be in both countries?

g. What are the labor supplies in each country after labor has been allowed to move?

h. What is the amount and direction of the labor movement?

i. What is the change in output in country I?

j. What is the change in output in country II?

k. What is the overall effect on total world output?

l. What happens to the overall effect on total world output if the L_2L_1 workers that moved to country II had been unemployed in country I before their migration?

CASE STUDY QUESTIONS
Refer to Case Study 1 (p.231) Determinants of Foreign Direct Investment

1. What factors appear to be positively related to foreign direct investment flows between developed countries? What factors are negatively related?

2. What factors appear to be most important to decisions to directly invest in developing nations?

3. Why is political stability important to investors considering developing countries but not on the list of factors for investments in developed nations?

4. Market size and the possibilities of economies of scale appear to be important in both cases. Explain why?

5. Discuss the importance of tariffs in determining the likelihood of foreign direct investment in a country.

6. Discuss the role of relative labor and capital costs, profits, and exchange rates in U.S. foreign direct investment.

Refer to Case Study 2 (p. 236) Possible Effects of Foreign Investment into the United States

1. What is the basis of the concern that "decisions that used to be made in Sacramento, Albany, and Washington, D.C., are now being made in Tokyo, London, and Riyadh."

2. Does the evidence support Mr. Prestowitz's claim that the U.S. is "a colony-in-the-making?" Why or why not?

3. Why are tax breaks or trade restrictions that benefit foreign investments in the U.S. potentially costly to the U.S.?

4. Are Graham and Krugman justified in concluding that the "alarm about the consequences of a growing foreign presence in the U.S. economy is not warranted?" Support your answer.

Refer to Case Study 3 (p. 242) Immigration into the United States and Canada

1. Some economists argue that the greater the difference between the wages in the source and host country the greater the probability of migration. Do Greenwood and McDowell's results support this argument? How?

2. Explain the relationship between "political rights" and the propensity to migrate to the U.S.

3. Could immigration policy have an effect on the difference in the relationship between higher education and migration in the two cases? How?

4. While this analysis suggests that many factors are of importance in the migration decision, do you believe that migration would continue to flow into the U.S. if wages were decreased on average by 50%? Explain your answer.

Refer to Case Study 4 (p. 244) "Foreign Medical Graduates Claim Licensing Bias"

1. How is this case related to the concept of "brain drain" discussed in this chapter?

2. What are the sources or methods of discrimination faced by foreign trained doctors?

3. Some consumer groups argue that the American Medical Association is more concerned with keeping salaries high than the availability of care. How is the handling of foreign medical graduates related to this claim?

4. If Congress passed a bill that prevented state licensing boards from discriminating against physicians trained abroad, would this end the discrimination discussed in this article? Why or why not?

ANSWERS

True/False Questions
1. False
2. False
3. False
4. True
5. True
6. True
7. False
8. True
9. True
10. False

Fill-in questions
1. branch plant
2. foreign subsidiary
3. Europe
4. market share
5. lowered
6. transfer pricing
7. performance requirements
8. abundance; lower; scarcity; higher
9. surplus
10. brain drain

Problems
1.
   a. Europe
   b. manufacturing, finance
   c. Europe
   d. manufacturing, wholesale trade

2.
   a. Ok_1
   b. $O'k_1$
   c. OO'
   d. Or_1
   e. $O'r_1'$
   f. capital will move from country II to country I in search of higher returns.
   g. return to capital drops from Or_1 to Or_2
   h. return to capital rises from $O'r_1'$ to $O'r_2'$
   i. k_2k_1 moves from country II to country I resulting in a new allocation of Ok_2 for country I's capital stock and $O'k_2$ for country II's capital stock.
   j. output in country I changes from $OACk_1$ to $OAEk_2$ rising by k_1CEk_2.
   k. output in country II changes from $O'A'C'k_1$ to $O'A'Ek_2$, falling by $k_1C'Ek_2$.

l.   total world output has increased because k_1CEk_2 is larger than $k_1C'Ek_2$. The increase is the area C'CE.

3.
a. OO'
b. OL_2
c. $O'L_2$
d. OW_1
e. OW_2 or O'F
f. OW_{eq}
g. OL_1 in country I and $O'L_1$ in country II.
h. L_2L_1 workers move from country I to country II in search of higher wages.
i. in country I output decreases by L_1ACL_2
j. in country II output rises by L_1ABL_2
k. the overall increase in output is CAB
l. the increase in output would be the entire area L_1ABL_2 because no output would be lost in country I as a result of the migration.

CHAPTER 13
The Instruments of Trade Policy

SUMMARY
Free trade in goods and services is disrupted with a wide variety of different devices. These protectionist devices serve to alter trade from its pattern of comparative advantage. The first device was a tax on imports or a tariff. Tariffs can charge a specified amount per unit (specific tariffs) or tax as a percentage of the value of the imported good (ad valorem tariffs).

In a world of trade distortions certain legislative actions work to insure tariff reductions for certain groups of producers. The Generalized System of Preferences (GSP) was designed to allow particular developing countries to export selected products to developed countries with no tariffs. Most Favored Nation (MFN) treatment assures nondiscrimination in that all nations with MFN status will receive tariff treatment equal to the best rate given to any other nation with MFN status.

When nations use tariffs as protectionist devices, the height of a country's average tariffs becomes a major concern. Average tariffs can be determined by taking an unweighted average tariff rate or a weighted average rate. The impact of tariffs on a nation's trade also involves the effective rate of protection (ERP). The ERP is the extent to which "value-added" in the domestic industry is altered by the entire tariff structure. Nations with escalated tariff structures have ERPs that exceed the nominal tariff rate on the final goods produced.

As the use of tariffs have been reduced by multinational negotiations, other less visible forms of trade barriers have taken their place. These new barriers are often referred to as nontariff barriers (NTBs) to trade. The first NTB discussed was an import quota. A quota is a direct quantity restriction that serves to limit the amount of a good imported during a specific time period. In recent years, Voluntary Export Restraints (VERs) have emerged as an alternative to quotas.

Many other NTBs are employed by governments to alter the free trade patter of resource allocation. These devices include:

> government procurement provisions
> domestic content provisions
> border tax adjustments
> administrative classifications
> restrictions on services
> trade related investment measures
> foreign exchange controls.

These devices along with many other forms of control affect the pattern of international trade. The welfare effects of these distortions will be examined in the next chapters.

DEFINE THE FOLLOWING KEY TERMS

ad valorem tariff (p. 249)

advance deposit requirements (p. 262)

domestic content provisions (p. 260)

effective tariff rate or effective rate of protection (ERP) (p. 256)

escalated tariff structure (p. 257)

export subsidy (p. 259)

export tax (p. 259)

Generalized System of Preferences (GSP) (p. 252)

government procurement provisions (p. 260)

import quota (p. 259)

import subsidies (p. 252)

most-favored-nation (MFN) treatment (p. 252)

nominal tariff rate (p. 256)

nontariff barriers (NTBs) (p. 259)

offshore assembly provisions (OAP) (p. 254)

preferential duties (p. 252)

prohibitive tariff (p. 255)

specific tariff (p. 249)

unweighted average tariff rate (p. 255)

"voluntary" export restraint (VER) or voluntary restraint agreement (VRA) (p. 260)

weighted average tariff rate (p. 255)

TRUE/FALSE QUESTIONS

1. An ad valorem tariff is levied as a constant percentage of the monetary value of one unit of the imported good.

2. An advantage of a specific tariff is that as an instrument of protection its protective value keeps pace with increases in the price of the import.

3. The Generalized System of Preferences is a system where a large number of developed nations permit duty-free entry of products from neighboring developed countries.

4. Under the offshore assembly provision, the tariff rate in practice on a good is lower than the tariff rate listed in the tariff schedules.

5. The weighted average tariff rate for a nation that imports a few goods with zero tariffs and has prohibitive tariffs on all other potential imports would be zero percent.

6. If the nominal tariff rate on the final good is lower than the weighted average nominal tariff rate on inputs, then the ERP will be higher than the nominal tariff rate on the final good.

7. An export subsidy is a payment to a firm by the government designed to increase the flow of trade of a country.

8. Provisions that restrict the purchasing of foreign products by government agencies are considered to be nontariff barriers.

9. Value-added tax rebates by Western European nations act as tariffs on American products entering Europe.

10. A country's choice to negotiate an administrative agreement with a foreign supplier whereby that supplier agrees to refrain from sending some exports to the importing country is known as a government procurement provision.

FILL-IN QUESTIONS

1. An import duty that assigns a fixed monetary tax per physical unit of the good imported is known as a _____ tariff.

2. A form of tariff legislation that represents an element of nondiscrimination in the application of tariff policy is _____ treatment.

3. Special treatment in terms of lower tariff rates applied to an import according to its geographical source is known as _____.

4. The _____ considers the tariff rates on each product weighted by the importance of the good in the total bundle of imports.

5. A tariff rate that is so high that it keeps imports from coming into the country is a _____ tariff.

6. The _____ tariff rate is the rate listed in a country's tariff schedule, while the _____ is the percentage change in the value added in a industry because of the imposition of a tariff structure by a country rather than the existence of free trade.

7. A system in which nominal tariff rates on imports of manufactured goods are higher than the nominal tariff rates on intermediate inputs and raw materials is an _____ structure.

8. An _____ specifies that only a certain physical amount of a good will be allowed into the country during a specific time period.

9. A policy that stipulates that a given percentage of the value of a good sold in the U.S. must consist of U.S. components or U.S. labor is a _____.

10. An importing country that has been preaching the virtues of free trade may choose to negotiate a _____ rather than a quota to restrict the quantity of imports.

DISCUSSION QUESTIONS

1. Define specific and ad valorem tariffs. Discuss the advantages and disadvantages of each type of duty.

2. Two major examples of preferential duties are the Generalized System of Preferences and Most Favored Nation treatment. Discuss the differences between the two policies including the preferential treatment provided by the GSP and nondiscriminatory treatment of the MFN status.

3. Compare and contrast the rationale and implementation of offshore assembly provisions and domestic content provisions.

4. Discuss the reasons for the downward bias in the calculation of the weighted average tariff rate. What are some possible adjustments to overcome this bias?

5. Domestic producers are seeking protection from foreign importers. Multinational negotiations have prohibited the use of tariffs and quotas. Discuss the advantages and disadvantages of the remaining protective devices available to the nation.

PROBLEMS

1. The following goods and associated tariffs are taken from the 1994 <u>Harmonized Tariff Schedule of the United States</u>.

Product	Tariff
sweet potatoes	10%
shelled almonds	$0.375 per kg.
frozen orange juice	$0.0925 per liter
ice cream	20%
toilet paper	5.3%
ballpoint pens	$0.08 each + 5.4%

   a. Identify the goods that are subject to a specific tariff.

   b. Identify the goods that are subject to an ad valorem tariff.

   c. Identify the good(s) that are subject to a combination tariff.

2. Assume a nation imports 3 goods with the following tariff rates:
   Good A, 10%
   Good B, 20%
   Good C, 30%.

   Suppose the nation imports the following amounts of each good:
   $100,000 worth of good A
   $300,000 worth of good B
   $600,000 worth of good C.

   a. Calculate the unweighted average tariff rate.

   b. Calculate the weighted average tariff rate.

c. Discuss adjustments that can be used to remove the potential downward bias in the weighted average rate.

3. Suppose the production of good X uses as intermediate inputs goods Y and Z which can be produced domestically or imported. Under free trade the prices of the three goods are as follows:

$$Good\ X \quad P_x = \$2500$$
$$Good\ Y \quad P_y = \$\ 500$$
$$Good\ Z \quad P_z = \$1000.$$

Domestic producers are successful in obtaining tariffs on the imports of the 3 goods. The tariff rates are as follows: $t_x = 20\%$, $t_y = 10\%$, $t_z = 5\%$

a. Find the value added in the final stage of production of good x under free trade.

b. Find the value added in the final stage of production of good x with tariffs in place.

c. Calculate the effective rate of protection (ERP).

4. The U.S. is importing computers from Malaysia at $1000 per computer. The tariff rate on computers is 20%. Suppose that the processing chip used in the Malaysian computers are U.S. components with a value of $400.

a. Determine the price paid by consumers (assuming the small country case) without an offshore assembly provision.

b. Determine the price paid by consumers if the Malaysian computer industry is operating under offshore assembly provisions.

c. Calculate the tariff rate as a percentage of import price under OAP.

CASE STUDY QUESTIONS
Refer to Case Study 1 (p. 250) U.S. Tariff Rates

1. From Table 1, identify the goods subject to the following:
   a. specific tariffs

   b. ad valorem tariffs

   c. combination tariffs.

2. From Table 1, identify the goods that have the largest increase in tariff rate as a result of a nation moving from MFN to non MFN status.

3. Discuss the impact of the U.S. negotiating an agreement to reduce the tariff on Italian ice cream to 10% on other nations with MFN status.

4. Analyze the potential impact of the removal of MFN status for Chinese exports to the U.S. Choose three items from Table 1 to demonstrate the size of the impact.

Refer to Case Study 2 (p. 253) The U.S. Generalized System of Preferences

1. Discuss the major advantage of being on the list of countries receiving GSP treatment from the U.S. Are there any additional benefits from obtaining "least developed" status?

2. Discuss the impact of Malaysia, Taiwan, South Korea, and Singapore graduating from GSP to MFN status.

3. Does GSP treatment assure that the eligible goods enter the U.S. without any restrictions? Why or why not?

Refer to Case Study 3 (p. 258) Nominal and Effective Tariffs in the U.S. and Japan

1. Discuss the difference between a nominal tariff rate and an effective tariff rate. Identify some reasons effective rates may be higher than the nominal tariff rates.

2. In the U.S. portion of Table 4, food, beverages, and tobacco rank tenth in nominal rates and move to fifth in effective rate. Discuss some potential reasons that this change is large relative to furniture and fixtures or miscellaneous manufactures.

3. In your opinion, what has happened to nominal and effective rates of tariff protection over the last 20 years in both nations?

4. Discuss the impact of including the protection provided by NTBs in the calculation of the effective rates of protection.

5. Do the industries included in the two lists and the effective rates of protection suggest that the U.S. and Japan have escalated tariff structures? Why or why not?

Refer to Case Study 4 (p. 262) Is It a Car? Is It a Truck?

1. Was the proposed reclassification of imported minivans and sport-utility vehicles from cars to trucks designed to reduce the U.S. budget deficit? Why or why not?

2. What groups stood to gain the most from the proposed reclassification? What groups would be adversely impacted by the change?

3. Explain why Suzuki was supporting a proposal that would raise the tariffs on its vehicles from 2.5% to 25%.

Refer to Case Study 5 (p. 264) Examples of Control over Trade

1. Discuss the impact of MERCOSUR membership on the Argentinean tariff structure. What is the role of exceptions in the transitional adjustment phase?

2. Discuss the use of health and religious controls as non-tariff barriers in Pakistan. What do you expect to happen to Pakistani prices as a result of these barriers.

3. Discuss some potential reasons for requiring import licenses to import goods from certain countries. What characteristics do these nations have in common? How do export licenses impact trade?

ANSWERS

True/False Questions
1. True
2. False
3. False
4. True
5. True
6. False
7. True
8. True
9. False
10. False

Fill-in questions
1. specific
2. most favored nation
3. preferential duties or preferential treatment
4. weighted average tariff rates
5. prohibitive
6. nominal; effective rate of protection
7. escalated tariff
8. import quota
9. domestic content provision
10. voluntary export restraint

Problems

1.   a.   shelled almonds, frozen orange juice
       b.   sweet potatoes, ice cream, toilet paper
       c.   ballpoint pens

2.   a. $\dfrac{10 + 20 + 30}{3} = \dfrac{60}{3} = 20\%$

       b. $\dfrac{(100{,}000)(10\%) + (300{,}000)(20\%) + (600{,}000)(30\%)}{100{,}000 + 300{,}000 + 600{,}000} =$

            $\dfrac{10{,}000 + 60{,}000 + 180{,}000}{100{,}000} = \dfrac{250{,}000}{100{,}000} = 25\%$

       c.   The tendency of higher tariff rates to discourage consumption of those goods causes a downward bias. Using world weights rather than a nation's own imports will help remove the bias.

3.   a.   2500 - (1000 + 500) = 2500 - 1500 = $1000
       b.   tariff prices   X = 2500 + (.2 x 2500) = 2500+500 = $3000
                             Y = 500 + (.1 x 500) = 500+50 = $550
                             Z = 1000 + (.05 x 1000) = 1000+50 = $1050

            value added $3000 - (550 + 1050) = 3000 - 1600 = $1400

       c.   ERP = $\dfrac{1400 - 1000}{1000} = \dfrac{400}{1000} = 40\%$

4.   a. $1000 + (.2 x $1000) = 1000 + 200 = $1200
       b. $1000 + (.2 x $600) = 1000 + 120 = $1120
       c.   120/1000 = 12%

CHAPTER 14
The Impact of Trade Policies

SUMMARY

The emphasis in previous chapters has been on the tools of trade policies. This chapter will focus on the costs and benefits associated with the use of trade distorting measures. The analysis will begin with a focus on the industry directly impacted by the policy using a partial equilibrium analysis. The analysis will then be expanded to consider the indirect effects beyond the one market with a general equilibrium analysis. The overall thrust is that there is a net social cost to the country that uses trade restrictions.

The partial equilibrium analysis will begin with the impacts of trade restrictions in an economically small country that is currently importing a product. The imposition of a tariff results in a higher domestic price for the imported good. This higher price results in a loss of consumer surplus, a gain in producer surplus for domestic producers and a gain in tariff revenue for the government. The consumer surplus loss exceeds the producer and government gains resulting in a net loss to society (deadweight losses) as a result of the tariff. The increase in domestic production and reduction in exports that the tariff provided could also be obtained with an import quota or a production subsidy. The welfare cost of the quota will equal or exceed that of the tariff depending upon the government's ability to capture the quota rent (equivalent to the tariff revenue). In the case of the subsidy, the incentive to increase domestic production is achieved without raising the prices paid by consumers. From a welfare standpoint, the subsidy is more attractive than a tariff or quota because there is no loss in consumer surplus and no deadweight loss for consumers. At this stage, the impact of the trade restriction on other related markets through cross-price effects is not considered. The total effects will be analyzed in the general equilibrium framework.

Trade restrictions aren't limited to imports, exports can be taxed, subsidized, and restricted with a quota. Export taxes and quotas are designed to discourage exports and lower domestic prices as producers expand domestic sales. In these cases producer surplus is reduced while consumer surplus and government tax revenues increase. The producer loss exceeds the gains by the consumers and government resulting in a net welfare loss. Due to the uncertainty of government collection of quota rent, the net welfare loss may be greater in the case of an export quota.

An export subsidy is designed to increase exports. The subsidy encourages producers to shift sales from the domestic market to exports. Producers gain from the subsidized prices and the increased production. Consumers are hurt by the higher prices and the government must pay the cost of the subsidy. Overall the costs exceed the producer gains causing a net welfare loss. The partial equilibrium analysis demonstrates the net welfare losses associated with policies designed to protect firms in the small country cases.

The second portion of the partial equilibrium analysis focuses on economically large countries. For these countries, changes in production or consumption can impact world prices of goods. The impact of trade restrictions in the large country scenario is measured using import demand schedules and export supply schedules. These schedules demonstrate quantity responses to price changes. The major change that occurs in this scenario is that the tariff may not be paid totally by the importing country. The burden may be shared by the importer and the exporter.

The sharing of the burden (or incidence) of the tariff is determined by the relative elasticities of export supply and import demand. The more elastic (price sensitive) the demand for imports relative to export supply, the greater the share of the tariff that is paid by the exporter. The ability to force the exporter to share a portion of the tariff burden means that the loss of consumer surplus is less for a large country and as a result the net cost of protection is less than for a small country. In the extreme, if the part of the tariff paid by the exporting country exceeded the consumer's part of the tariff, a large country could experience a net welfare gain. This result is only possible under the assumption that there is no retaliation from the exporting country.

The large country scenario is also used to analyze quotas and voluntary export restraints (VER). Once again, if the government obtains all of the quota rent a quota is equivalent to a tariff. The VER is equivalent to a quota in which the government receives no quota rent. The net welfare effect for the VER is then unambiguously negative.

If the large country seeks to impact exports with subsidies and taxes, the burden of the policy must be examined. A large country can use an export tax to reduce supply and increase the world price. The burden of the tax is shared by the foreign buyer and the domestic producer. In the absence of retaliation, the increase in the export price can improve the country's terms of trade leading to a positive welfare effect. In the case of an export subsidy, home consumers are injured as producers shift more goods into exports. In addition, the lack of a tax to raise international prices and be shared by foreign consumers creates an extra loss for the large country. The export subsidy has no potential welfare gain to offset the deadweight losses.

Moving from the partial equilibrium to the general equilibrium framework allows an examination of impacts on the whole economy. In the small country case, the impact of a tariff or quota are seen in the distortion of domestic prices. Artificially raising the price of one good relative to others forces the economy to an inferior production point. The potential consumption associated with the new production point is on a lower indifference curve than before the restriction indicating a loss in overall welfare. A subsidy has the advantage of not distorting the prices but the production shift still reduces overall welfare.

The large country general equilibrium analysis uses offer curves. The reduction in welfare associated with tariffs and quotas are at least partially offset by improvements in the TOT for the large country. The use of a VER results in a depreciation in the TOT increasing the negative impact from the trade barrier. Once again, it must be considered that any improvements in the TOT are in the absence of retaliation.

Lastly, there are a few additional impacts of protection that must be mentioned. Any policy to restrict imports will likely lead to a reduction in exports either from retaliation or factor redistribution. Also, trade restrictions impact on income distribution which must be considered. A reduction in the imports of a good may actually lead to increased imports of parts to supply the domestic import-competitor. Overall, increases in the level of protection bring greater net welfare losses.

DEFINE THE FOLLOWING KEY TERMS

auction quota system (p. 271)

consumer surplus (p. 268)

cross-price effects (p. 273)

deadweight losses (p. 270)

demand for imports schedule (p. 278)

equivalent quota (p. 271)

equivalent subsidy (p. 272)

equivalent tariff (p. 271)

general equilibrium model (p. 267)

incidence of the tariff (p. 281)

partial equilibrium analysis (p. 267)

producer surplus (p. 268)

supply of exports schedule (p. 278)

TRUE/FALSE QUESTIONS

1. In a small country partial equilibrium analysis, the increase in producer surplus plus the government revenue from a tariff are greater than the loss of consumer surplus.

2. In a small country partial equilibrium analysis, the welfare effects of equivalent tariffs and quotas are the same if the government captures the entire quota rent.

3. From a welfare standpoint, a subsidy is preferred to a tariff because there is no consumer surplus loss in the small country partial equilibrium model.

4. The imposition of an export tax is designed to increase the domestic price causing producers to expand domestic sales.

5. The importing country might benefit from the imposition of an export quota if it can acquire enough of the quota rent.

6. The demand for imports schedule will generally be less elastic than the demand for the good itself.

7. For the large country, the increase in the domestic price of a good is greater than for a small country resulting in a greater loss of consumer surplus and net welfare.

8. In the large country case, the welfare effect for the home country from the VER is thus a loss equal to the loss from an equivalent import quota when the foreign exporters capture the quota rent.

9. In the general equilibrium analysis for a small country, the imposition of a VER has the impact of raising the price of the restricted good to the importing country thus worsening the importing country's terms of trade.

10. Faced with import barriers, foreign firms may devote even more time and resources to reducing the costs of production, thereby, becoming an even stronger competitor.

FILL-IN QUESTIONS

1. _____ refers to the area bounded by the demand curve on top and the market price below.

2. The net costs to society of distorting the domestic free-trade market price with a tariff are the _____.

3. A system of competitive bidding in which the licenses to import goods under a quota are sold by the government is called an _____.

4. In the case of nonhomogeneous goods, the impact of a price distortion in a given market can extend into other markets by means of _____.

5. In a small country, the imposition of an export tax directly raises/lowers the price received by the producer for exported units of the product.

6. The derivation of a country's export supply schedule uses the fact that exports are equal to _____ minus _____.

7. The extent to which the tariff is paid by one party or the other, the _____, depends importantly on the slope of the S_m schedule.

8. A large country is less able to shift the cost of the tariff to the exporting country when domestic demand and supply become more _____ and the exporting country's demand and supply become more _____.

9. In the general equilibrium analysis, the imposition of a tariff in the absence of retaliation results in an _____ of the nations terms-of-trade.

10. The restriction of imports is likely to lead to a _____ in exports of the tariff-imposing country as a result of factor reallocation and potential retaliation.

DISCUSSION QUESTIONS

1. In the small country partial equilibrium case, compare and contrast the welfare effects of an import tariff, an import quota, and a subsidy to import competing production.

2. Consider the impact of a tariff in a market with nonhomogeneous goods. Discuss the cross-price effects and the welfare changes in the markets.

3. Compare and contrast the net welfare effects of an export tax and an export quota in the small country partial equilibrium case.

4. Discuss the impact of an export subsidy on domestic production, domestic consumption, and overall welfare.

5. In the large country partial equilibrium analysis, discuss the relationship between the incidence of a tariff and the relative elasticities of export supply and import demand. Develop a case where the greater incidence of the tariff falls on the exporter.

6. Compare the net welfare effects of trade restrictions between the large country analysis and the small country analysis.

7. Discuss the potential allocation of the rent associated with the imposition of a quota to the government, the exporter, and the importer.

8. In the small country general equilibrium analysis the net costs of protection on a country would be ranked as subsidy < tariff < = quota. Do you agree or disagree? Explain.

9. In the large country general equilibrium analysis, improvements in the terms-of-trade are supposed to offset the reductions in welfare associated with the use of tariffs, quotas, and VERs. Is this true in all three cases? Explain.

10. "In the long run, protection may impair the protected country's competitiveness and encourage innovation abroad." Explain how this may be one of the unintended results of protectionism.

PROBLEMS
1. In reference to Figure 3 on page 269, identify the following:
    a. total consumption prior to the tariff

    b. domestic production prior to the tariff

    c. imports prior to the tariff

    d. total consumption after the tariff

    e. domestic production after the tariff

    f. imports after the tariff

    g. consumer surplus loss as a result of the tariff

    h. producer surplus gain as a result of the tariff

    i. government revenue generated by the tariff

    j. deadweight losses as a result of the tariff

2. Using Figure 4 on page 272, identify the following:
   a. total domestic consumption prior to the subsidy or tariff

   b. total domestic production prior to the subsidy or tariff

   c. imports prior to the subsidy or tariff

   If price remains at $5.00 ($P_{int}$) and a subsidy shifts supply to S_1, identify the following:

   d. domestic production with the subsidy

   e. total consumption with the subsidy

   f. imports with the subsidy

   g. taxpayer cost of the subsidy

   h. increase in producer surplus from the subsidy

   i. deadweight loss from the subsidy

   j. is the net welfare loss greater in the case of the tariff or the subsidy.

3. Using Figure 12 on page 284, identify the following:

   a. the price of the good in free trade

   b. the size of the quota imposed

   c. the quota adjusted import supply schedule

   d. price paid by consumers after the quota

   e. price received by the exporter

   f. quota rent

   g deadweight loss.

CASE STUDY QUESTIONS
Refer to Case Study 1 (p. 275) The Effects of Protection in the U.S. Textile Industry

1. What is the origin of the Multifiber Arrangement (MFA)?

2. What groups are being protected by the MFA? What groups are being hurt by the MFA?

3. Using the information in Table 1, determine the consumer welfare loss and net welfare loss per job saved in 1986 and 1990.

4. Has the protection provided by the MFA resulted in improvements by American textile and apparel manufacturers that have made them more competitive? Discuss the overall results of the MFA.

Refer to Case Study 2 (p.285) Welfare Costs of U.S. Import Quotas/VERs

1. In the case of U.S. VERs what group tends to capture the quota rents?

2. How was the total U.S. welfare loss calculated? Given the distribution of the quota rents, how does this loss compare to that of equivalent tariffs?

3. Compare the total U.S. welfare loss with the total world welfare loss from these restrictions. Who is paying the cost of these restrictions? Are they effective? Explain.

4. Given the information in this case, what policy suggestions do you have for the U.S. automobile, sugar, textiles and apparel, diary products, and steel industries?

Refer to Case Study 3 (p. 289) The U.S. Export Enhancement Program for Wheat

1. Discuss the purposes of the Export Enhancement Program for Wheat. Why is the "additionality" criteria important?

2. Who are the major "winners" as a result of the implementation of this program? What groups are considered to be losers?

3. Does the EEP program seem to be meeting the 4 criteria set out by the Economic Policy Council of the White House? Why or why not?

Refer to Case Study 4 (p. 296) Domestic Effects of the Sugar Quota System

1. Discuss the potential indirect effects of the sugar quota system on firms that use sugar as an input. Be sure to consider the impact on employment, profitability, investment, and international competitiveness.

2. List and explain some of the noneconomic costs that are associated with the sugar quota system.

3. Discuss the income distribution effects of the sugar quota program.

4. How does a program such as this manage to continue for over 60 years? Discuss the relative power of the winners and losers from these restrictions.

ANSWERS

True/False Questions
1. False
2. True
3. True
4. False
5. True
6. False
7. False
8. True
9. True
10. True

Fill-in questions
1. consumer surplus
2. deadweight losses
3. auction quota system
4. cross price effects
5. raises
6. home production; home consumption
7. incidence of the tariff
8. inelastic; elastic
9. appreciation or improvement
10. reduction

Problems
1. a. 190 units
   b. 100 units
   c. 90 units
   d. 160 units
   e. 120 units
   f. 40 units
   g. ABFH
   h. ABCJ
   i. KCFG
   j. JCK and GFH

2. a. 190 units
   b. 100 units
   c. 90 units
   d. 120 units
   e. 190 units
   f. 70 units
   g. ABCK

      h.   ABCJ
      i.   JCK
      j.   the loss is greater in the tariff case due to the additional consumer loss from the price increase.

3   a. P_{m0}
      b. Q_{m1}
      c. RFS'_m
      d. P_{m1}
      e. P_{m2}
      f. $P_{m2}P_{m1}E'F$
      g.   GE'E

CHAPTER 15
Traditional Arguments for Protection

SUMMARY

There are several arguments for protection that have a long history of influence on policymakers and the general public. The arguments are analyzed individually and discussed in terms of alternative policies to achieve trade objectives. In all cases, we must understand the perspective from which the argument for protection is put forth in order to have meaningful discussions.

The first argument for protection is concerned with enhancing the welfare of the world as a whole. The infant industry argument is based on the existence of a new industry that has the potential to become a low-cost world producer. The threat of low-cost imports from foreign competition may prevent the development of this industry unless protection is provided during the start-up period.

A second set of arguments are based on improving national well-being. The first in this group is the terms of trade argument for protection. While acknowledging a decline in world welfare, this argument suggests that the imposition of a tariff will result in gains in the home country's welfare. This argument is a beggar-my-neighbor argument and may result in retaliation by the injured nation.

The second argument based on improving national well being is a tariff to reduce aggregate unemployment. The argument suggests that domestic unemployment will be reduced as a tariff shifts the demand of consumers from foreign goods to home-produced goods. There is no certainty that the tariff will accomplish the desired goal and economists stress that there are other policies better able to achieve the goal.

The next group of arguments are based on the improvement of an individual industry or factor. This group includes arguments for tariffs to increase employment in a particular industry, to offset foreign dumping, to offset foreign subsidies, and to benefit a scarce factor of production. These arguments all emphasize the welfare of a particular group over national welfare or international efficiency. Economists also question whether a tariff is the best method of achieving the industry specific goals.

The final two arguments also based on improving national well-being are the national defense argument and the improving the balance of trade argument. The national defense argument suggests that if international trade drives critical domestic industries out of the market, national security may be threatened. In addition to the difficulties identifying industries vital to national defense, other policies may have the desired impact with a lower welfare cost. The balance of trade argument for tariffs does not guarantee balanced trade and may not be the appropriate way to address an essentially macroeconomic phenomenon.

The range of arguments for protection are designed to benefit groups as divergent as the whole world and owners of a particular factor of production. In almost all cases welfare-superior alternatives to tariffs exist if there is a desire to achieve the specific objective.

DEFINE THE FOLLOWING KEY TERMS

antidumping argument (p. 308)

antidumping duty (p. 309)

beggar-my-neighbor policy (p. 302)

countervailing duty (CVD) (p. 311)

dumping (p. 308)

infant industry argument (p. 299)

macroeconomic interpretation of a trade deficit (p. 313)

national defense argument (p. 311)

optimum tariff rate (p. 303)

persistent dumping (p. 309)

predatory dumping (p. 309)

specificity principle (p. 307)

sporadic dumping (p. 309)

tariff to benefit a scarce factor of production (p. 311)

tariff to improve the balance of trade (p. 312)

tariff to increase employment in a particular industry (p. 307)

tariff to offset a foreign subsidy (p. 309)

tariff to reduce aggregate unemployment (p. 306)

terms-of-trade argument (p. 302)

TRUE/FALSE QUESTIONS
1. The argument for infant industry protection is based on the belief that the infant industry will be able to recognize sufficient economies of scale to mature into a low cost world producer.

2. A nation experiencing high rates of unemployment during a recession may use a tariff to shift consumption from home-produced goods to foreign goods and thereby decrease unemployment.

3. Tariffs to increase employment in a particular industry are the welfare-superior means to save jobs in the industry.

4. Dumping occurs when a firm sells its product at a lower price in the export market than in the home market.

5. While an export subsidy allows a country to export a product without a comparative advantage, world welfare is reduced because of the distortion.

6. The tariff to benefit a scarce factor of production allows the owners of the scarce factor of production and the producing nation to gain at the expense of world efficiency.

7. The national defense argument has been used to protect the U.S. watch industry, clothespin industry, and even the garlic producers.

8. A tariff to improve the balance of trade focuses on increasing exports while keeping the level of imports constant.

9. If an industry is correctly identified as qualifying for infant industry protection, a subsidy has a lower welfare cost to the country than a tariff.

10. A tariff to reduce aggregate unemployment will not be successful if jobs saved in import-competing industries are offset by job losses in export industries.

FILL-IN QUESTIONS

1. The _____ argument for tariff protection is based on the belief that certain industries are vital to a nation's security.

2. The _____ argument for tariff protection is based on the belief that protection given to an industry in the early stages of production will allow the industry to realize sufficient economies of scale to be an international competitor.

3. The terms-of-trade argument for protection acknowledges that home country gains in welfare will be offset by losses of welfare in other countries and is thus a _____ policy.

4. A major problem with the terms-of-trade argument for protection is the fact that the injured trading partner may _____ with a tariff of its own.

5. Given a desire to increase employment in a particular industry, a _____ is a welfare-superior way to attain the goal rather than a tariff.

6. The belief that a tariff will shift demand by domestic consumers from foreign goods to home-produced goods resulting in greater domestic production and employment is the basis of the _____ argument for protection.

7. A foreign firm selling at a low price until home producers are driven out of the market in order to attain a monopoly position in the market is an example of _____.

8. The federal agency that determines whether dumping has been an important source of injury to the import-competing industry is the _____.

9. As a nation becomes more concerned with its trade deficit, the request for a tariff to reduce the amount of imports is based on the argument for a tariff to _____.

10. The tariff rate that maximizes a country's welfare is known as the _____ rate.

DISCUSSION QUESTIONS

1. Discuss the difficulties associated with the identification of industries that are likely to realize economies of scale and become low cost producers. What problems can result from infant industry protection being given to the wrong firms?

2. Using the simple formula from page 303, discuss the relationship between a country I's optimal tariff rate and the elasticity of import demand for country II.

3. When a tariff is used to reduce aggregate unemployment, the focus is on shifting domestic demand from imports to domestically produced goods. Discuss the reasons that jobs may be lost as a side-effect of this tariff.

4. Outline the procedures involved in the U.S. government's response to claims of dumping. Discuss the difficulties associated with determining whether persistent, predatory, or sporadic dumping has occurred.

5. Protection to benefit a scarce factor of production is an income redistribution issue. Discuss the costs associated with using a tariff to meet this objective and the more economically efficient means to accomplish this goal.

6. The use of a tariff to improve the balance of trade has many political and economic repercussions. Discuss these repercussions and the end result of the tariff policy when the repercussions are taken into account.

7. In many of the cases discussed in this chapter a tariff was not the best means to accomplish a particular objective. Discuss the benefits of using a subsidy over a tariff in the cases of infant industry protection, increasing aggregate employment, and national defense protection.

PROBLEMS

1. Given the simple formula for the relationship between the optimal tariff rate (t_I^*) and the elasticity of the foreign country's offer curve:

   $$t_I^* = 1/e_{II} - 1.$$

   a. Calculate the optimal tariff rate if $e_{II} = 4.0$.

   b. Calculate the optimal tariff rate if $e_{II} = 6.0$.

   c. What do these results demonstrate about the relationship between t_I^* and e_{II}?

2. Assume the U.S. trade figures are as follows:
   Imports $550 billion
   Exports $450 billion.

   a. Calculate the U.S. trade balance.

   b. Is this balance a surplus or deficit?

   c. Describe the use of a tariff to improve the balance of trade and some major problems associated with the policy.

CASE STUDY QUESTIONS
Refer to Case Study 1 (p. 301) U.S. Motorcycles -- A Successful Infant Industry?

1. How did an industry that had been in business since 1901 qualify for infant industry protection?

2. Describe the type of infant industry protection afforded Harley-Davidson. What aspect of this protection package assured that the government was not setting up permanent protection for an industry that would never be internationally competitive?

3. What was the cost to consumers of protection in terms of higher motorcycle prices? What was the cost per job saved? What two groups were primarily affected by those costs?

4. Was the infant industry protection a success in the Harley-Davidson case? Outline arguments for both sides of this issue.

Refer to Case Study 2 (p. 305) Terms of Trade Effects of U.S. and Japanese Tariffs

1. Discuss the reasons that at bilateral 10% increase in tariffs by the U.S. has a much larger impact on Japan's real income than a multilateral 10% increase in tariffs by the U.S.

2. Petri's study does not account for the possible impact of retaliatory tariffs by the exporting nations. Given your understanding of the impact of tariffs to improve the balance of trade, what do you predict would happen to U.S. real income if the 10% multilateral tariff was matched by retaliatory tariffs in each nation? Why?

3. Using Petri's estimates, what would be the outcome of a trade war in which the U.S. and Japan both placed 10% tariffs on all imports from the other nation? Discuss the impact on overall trade and the welfare of the world as a whole.

Refer to Case Study 3 (p. 308) Costs of Protecting Industry Employment

1. Assuming the average worker in these industries is paid a salary of $32,000 per year, convert the consumer cost per job saved into the multiples of the average worker's salary spent to preserve each job. (i.e. costume jewelry 96,000/32,000 = 3 times the average worker's salary). How are these costs justified?

2. Describe the impact of these policies on the following groups:
   a. U.S. Consumers

   b. U.S. Producers that use these products as inputs

   c. Foreign Producers

   d. U.S. Exporters

   e. The U.S. economy as a whole.

3. Discuss the reasons that it may be more politically acceptable to pay these high costs per job saved than to make a direct monetary payment to displaced workers.

Refer to Case Study 4 (p. 310) Recent Antidumping Actions

1. In order to implement antidumping tariffs, what findings are necessary from investigations by the U.S. Department of Commerce and the USITC?

2. In the case of Korean memory chips, how would you explain the differential duties applied to the four producers?

3. In the case of Canadian carbon steel imports, what circumstances could account for the determination that the carbon steel exports from the U.S. were not injuring Canadian producers?

4. If these three cases are assumed to be predatory dumping, discuss the impact on resource movements and long-run prices for the goods.

ANSWERS

True/False Questions
1. True
2. False
3. False
4. True
5. True
6. False
7. True
8. False
9. True
10. True

Fill-in questions
1. national defense
2. infant industry
3. beggar-my-neighbor
4. retaliate
5. subsidy to employment
6. tariff to reduce aggregate unemployment
7. predatory dumping
8. U.S. International Trade Commission
9. improve the balance of trade
10. optimal tariff

Problems
1. a. $t_I^* = 1/4 - 1 = 1/3 = 33.3\%$
   b. $t_I^* = 1/6 - 1 = 1/5 = 20\%$
   c. These results indicate that the larger the elasticity of foreign demand (more elastic) the smaller the optimal tariff rate.

2. a. exports - imports = $450 - $550 = -$100 billion
   b. balance of payments deficit
   c. The imposition of a tariff is designed to reduce imports and assuming exports are not affected decrease the balance of payments deficit. This policy ignores a variety of repercussions (such as retaliation) that will decrease exports reducing the improvement in trade balance and decreasing world welfare.

CHAPTER 16
Strategic Approaches to Trade Policy Intervention

SUMMARY

In recent years, economists have attempted to develop theories that demonstrate potential gains from tariffs or other trade restrictions. These models have focused on imperfectly competitive industries. The major change that occurs is that imperfect competition results in recognized interdependence between the firms. In the examination of these models it is very difficult to determine if protection will ultimately benefit a nation.

The first case examines a tariff to extract foreign monopoly profit. Under the assumption that a nation is totally dependent on a foreign monopoly to supply a particular good, a tariff is used to extract some of the monopoly profit. The tariff will raise the monopolist's marginal cost, reduce its exports, and increase the price paid by consumers. Consumers experience a reduction in their consumer surplus and the government gains the tariff revenue. If the gain in tariff revenue exceeds the lost consumer surplus, the importing nation has increased its welfare at the expense of the foreign monopolist and world welfare and efficiency.

The second case considers two competing firms from two different nations (a duopoly). The firms exhibit recognized interdependence and economies of scale in production. The interdependence between the two firms suggest that increased sales by one firm reduces the profit opportunities and therefore sales of the other firm. Each firm has an incentive to increase production and sales to realize economies of scale. A tariff by the home country allows the domestic firm to increase output and lower marginal costs causing the foreign firm to reduce output and experience increases in marginal cost. As a result of the changes in marginal cost, the domestic firm increases sales in all markets while the foreign firm experiences decreases in sales. This model is not advanced as an argument for protection. Protection of this type would probably be matched with a retaliatory tariff offsetting market share gains and reducing the volume of trade.

The third model also consists of two firms from two different nations. In this case, marginal cost depends on the level of research and development (R & D). A tariff by the home country government will reserve a larger share of the home market for the domestic firm. The increase in output stimulates a greater amount of R & D spending which lowers marginal cost. The cost reduction allows the domestic firm to take sales away from the foreign firm in all markets. Once again, the possibility of retaliation must be considered in assessing this argument.

The final model considers a home firm and a foreign firm competing for sales in a third country. The use of a subsidy to enhance a home firms exports can be explained with the use of a "payoff matrix". The four possible solutions indicate that the market is not large enough for both firms to produce the good economically. The only chance to make a positive profit is if one firm produces and the other does not produce. A subsidy to the home firm that is announced by the government will lead the home firm to commit to greater production and sales. The foreign firm will also realize the need to reduce its own sales. The home country can gain if the producer surplus gains from increased sales outweigh the cost of the subsidy. Once again these gains come at the expense of the foreign country's welfare and there is no guarantee that the foreign government will not offer its own subsidy.

While the new approaches may judge that imperfect competition better represents the world around us, the models are not designed as recommendations for protection. In making an assessment of these arguments, the opportunity costs of resources given up by other industries in order to support expansion and the possibility of retaliation must be considered.

DEFINE THE FOLLOWING KEY TERMS
duopoly (p. 317)

export subsidy in duopoly (p. 322)

imperfect competition (p. 315)

reaction functions (p. 317)

recognized interdependence (p. 315)

tariff to extract foreign monopoly profit (p. 315)

tariff to promote exports through economies of scale (p. 320)

tariff to promote exports through research and development (p. 320)

TRUE/FALSE QUESTIONS

1. Recognized interdependence is a characteristic of firms in a perfectly competitive industry.

2. A monopolist differs from a perfectly competitive firm because its marginal revenue is less than price.

3. A tariff on a foreign monopolist increases its marginal cost decreasing output produced and the price charged.

4. A model that assumes an industry is made up of two firms is known as a duopoly.

5. In a duopoly framework with economies of scale, the reaction function for the home firm indicates that increases in foreign firm sales will be matched by increases in home firm sales.

6. In a duopoly framework with economies of scale, a tariff by the home country on the foreign firms goods will allow the home firm to increase output pushing up marginal cost and price to the tariff level.

7. In considering a tariff to promote exports through research and development, the relationship between marginal cost and research and development expenditures is assumed to be negative.

8. Collie (1991) found the potential use of a countervailing duty by a foreign country is likely to encourage the home country to subsidize the home firms exports.

9. If home consumption is allowed in an export subsidy model in duopoly, the export subsidy will lower prices to home consumers and thereby increase consumer welfare.

10. Krugman's (1984) contribution to "new protectionism" was to demonstrate how import protection for one firm with economies of scale leads to an increase in exports for the protected firm in any foreign market in which that firm operates.

FILL-IN QUESTIONS

1. _____ refers to the tendency of imperfectly competitive firms to attempt to take into account the reactions of other firms in deciding their best course of action.

2. In Krugman's (1984) duopoly framework, the assumption that the firm's marginal cost declines with an increase in output indicates that _____ are associated with producing the output.

3. In Krugman's (1984) economies of scale in a duopoly framework, the interdependence suggests that the firm's revenue depends _____ on its own output but _____ on the foreign firm's output.

4. In Brander & Spencer's (1981) case where a foreign firm is the only supplier of a product in the world market a tariff is suggested to _____.

5. A tariff on a foreign monopoly is expected to _____ the monopoly profit, _____ tariff revenue for the domestic government, and _____ consumer surplus.

6. The use of a tariff to promote exports through economies of scale is expected to increase the market share for the domestic firm. The increased production and sales will _____ marginal cost for the home firm causing sales by the domestic firm to _____ in each export market.

7. In the tariff to promote exports through research and development model, Krugman assumes that the firm's marginal cost is _____ related to research and development expenditures.

Use the following payoff matrix to answer questions 8-10.

		Firm F Produces	Firm F Does Not Produce
Firm H	Produces	-50 / -50	$0 / $500
	Does not Produce	$500 / $0	$0 / $0

8. If both firms produce the good, production by Firm H will result in a _____ while production by Firm F will result in a _____.

9. If Firm F produces and Firm H does not produce, payoff for Firm F is _____ while payoff for Firm H is _____.

10. Firm H's government offers a subsidy of $100 if it produces for the world market. The subsidy will result in a payoff of _____ for Firm H if both firms produce and a payoff of _____ is Firm H is the only producer.

DISCUSSION QUESTIONS

1. The strategic approach to trade policy intervention base the potential gains on the absence of retaliation. Do you believe this is a realistic condition? How would retaliation impact the potential gains of the domestic firm and the welfare of the world?

2. In the use of a tariff to extract foreign monopoly profit, discuss the groups that gain welfare and those that experience welfare losses. What type of domestic redistribution would be necessary to offset the welfare losses?

3. Using Krugman's economies of scale in a duopoly framework, discuss the major assumptions and the resulting reaction functions. What condition is necessary for stability?

4. Using Krugman's economies of scale in a duopoly framework, explain the impact of a tariff on imports of the foreign firm on:
   home firm domestic market share
   home firm production
   home firm marginal cost
   home firm sales in foreign markets
   foreign firm production
   foreign firm marginal cost
   foreign firm sales in export markets.

5. In the tariff to promote exports through research and development model discuss the following:
    the assumed relationship between R & D expenditures and marginal cost
    the potential costs of inducing more resources into the R & D oriented industry with a tariff.

6. Given a duopoly framework with a home firm and a foreign firm competing in a third market that is not large enough for both firms to produce the good economically. Discuss the role of an export subsidy in landing credibility to a decision to expand sales. Analyze the impact of a countervailing duty to offset the subsidy.

PROBLEMS

1. Using Figure 1 on page 316, answer the following questions.
   a. identify the pre-tariff price and quantity

   b. identify the post-tariff price and quantity

   c. identify the tariff revenue collected by the government

   d. identify the foreign monopolist's post-tariff profit

   e. identify the reduction in domestic consumer surplus.

2. Given the following payoff matrixes

		Firm F		
		Produces		Does not produce
Firm H	Produces	-$100 -$100		$0 $1000
	Does not Produce	$1000 $0		$0 $0

Identify the payoff for Firm F in the following cases:
a. both firms produce

b. only Firm F produces

c. Firm F does not produce

Identify the payoff for Firm H in the following cases:
d. both firms produce

e. only firm H produces

f. Firm H does not produce

g. What subsidy would be necessary to assure production by Firm H and why?

CASE STUDY QUESTIONS
Refer to Case Study 1 (p.323) "Targeting" of Industries in Japan

1. Identify some of the measures used by the Japanese government to assist targeted industries.

2. Discuss the actions taken by the U.S. government to offset the success experienced by Japanese exporters.

3. Is the Japanese government an example of the government doing a better job of picking winning industries than the market forces? Why or why not?

4. Do you believe that the Japanese experience with targeting industries suggests the U.S. should adopt a similar industrial policy? Explain your answer.

Refer to Case Study 2 (p. 327) Airbus Industrie

1. Within the export subsidy in duopoly framework, explain the heavy European subsidization of Airbus Industrie.

2. The foreign firm competing with Airbus Industrie is Boeing Company of the United States. Discuss the U.S. response to the European subsidy.

3. Given the results of Richard Baldwin's analysis, what was the payoff when both firms produce? Do these results support the conclusion that "strategic trade policy" only benefits the countries who don't engage in it? Explain.

ANSWERS

True/False Questions
1. False
2. True
3. False
4. True
5. False
6. False
7. True
8. False
9. False
10. True

Fill-in questions
1. recognized interdependence
2. economies of scale
3. positively; negatively
4. extract foreign monopoly profit
5. decrease; increase; decrease
6. decrease; increase
7. negatively (or inversely)
8. loss of 50 dollars, loss of 50 dollars
9. $500, $0
10. $50, $600

Problems
1. a. price = Op_1 quantity = Oq_1
   b. price = Op_2 quantity = Oq_2
   c. tariff revenue = c_1c_2GH
   d. post-tariff profit = c_2p_2SG
   e. lost consumer surplus = p_1p_2SR

2. a. - $100
   b. $1000
   c. $0
   d. - $100
   e. $1000
   f. $0
   g. a subsidy of over $100 would assure firm H of a positive payoff from producing regardless of Firm F's decision.

CHAPTER 17
Political Economy and Recent U.S. Trade Policy

SUMMARY

This chapter begins by addressing the impact of institutions and the political process on U.S. trade policy. While the vast majority of economists agree that free trade is beneficial to a country, trade policy is influenced by individuals and groups that believe that they will be better off with restricted trade.

The first, and perhaps the most pervasive, political factor in the formation of trade policy is the economic self-interest of political participants. Through the influence of interest groups and funding political campaigns a small group of individuals who stand much to gain may have a greater impact on political policy than a large group of diverse consumers who stand to lose with protectionism.

A second political factor in the formation of trade policy is social concerns. Trade policy may be part of a larger policy package that is being used to promote social goals such as income distribution, increased productivity, economic growth, national defense, or global leadership. The policies could also be influenced by foreign policy goals such as promoting growth in developing countries or strengthening the non-communist world. In either case, the determination of trade policy is much more difficult than finding the option that increases the welfare of the majority of the population.

Trade policy of the last sixty years has been dominated by trade liberalization in the United States and other industrial countries. This period of trade liberalization began after the failure of the Tariff Act of 1930. Bilateral attempts to reduce tariffs began with the Reciprocal Trade Agreements Act of 1934. Significant reductions in tariff rates were achieved and then after WWII the move to multilateral negotiations allowed even greater progress.

The General Agreement on Tariffs and Trade (GATT) took effect in 1947. GATT has become the ongoing organization that sponsors regular negotiations to reduce trade barriers. The first five series of negotiations (known as rounds) were somewhat successful in reducing various trade barriers. In 1962, the Kennedy Round of trade negotiations were marked by a major breakthrough - the replacement of item-by-item negotiations with across-the-board tariff reductions. This breakthrough allowed negotiators from the 70 participating nations to reduce tariffs on manufactured goods by an average of 35 percent.

The success of the Kennedy round began to be offset by increases in NTBs. In 1974, the Tokyo Round of Trade negotiations began to address these threats to trade liberalization. They achieved further reductions in tariffs on manufactured goods, set up codes of behavior concerning NTBs, and established preferential treatment for certain exports from developing nations.

In 1986, the Uruguay Round of trade negotiations were initiated to further efforts to liberalize trade. The Uruguay Round continued to focus on NTBs while expanding to discuss service trade and removal of restrictions on agricultural trade. In December 1993, 117 nations reached agreement and began the move toward even greater liberalization. Briefly, the agreement continued to cut tariffs, made significant progress toward reducing agricultural subsidies, moved textiles and apparel into the GATT framework, and obtained "national treatment" for services. Finally, the agreement replaced GATT with a new organization known as the World Trade Organization (WTO).

While the general trend has certainly been toward greater trade liberalization, not all U.S. trade policy has been designed to remove trade restrictions. The 1980's were a period of Voluntary Export Restraints to protect automobile and steel producers. Other trade initiatives such as the Omnibus Trade and Competitiveness Act of 1988 and the Strategic Impediments Initiative included clauses designed to overcome "unfair" trading practices of other nations. These initiatives have been part of a return to greater bilateralism in trade negotiations. This shift toward "results based" country specific policies is sometimes referred to as a form of industrial policy or managed trade. A substantial debate has arisen around intellectual property protection, labor standards, and environmental legislation in countries exporting to the U.S.

While pressure for a more interventionist or managed approach to trade will never end, the general trend since 1934 has certainly been toward trade liberalization. A major indication of continued movement in the direction of liberalization came in the form of the 1993 adoption of the North American Free Trade Agreement (NAFTA).

DEFINE THE FOLLOWING KEY TERMS
across-the-board approach (p. 337)

bilateral negotiations (p. 336)

consumer subsidy equivalent (CSE) (p. 341)

directly unproductive activity (p. 333)

fast-track procedure (p. 340)

GATT rounds of trade negotiations (p. 337)

General Agreement on Tariffs and Trade (GATT) (p. 337)

Helms-Burton Law (p. 347)

industrial policy (p. 349)

item-by-item approach (p. 336)

Kennedy Round of trade negotiations (p. 337)

managed trade (p. 349)

median-voter model (p. 332)

multilateral negotiations (p. 336)

"new reciprocity" approach to trade policy (p. 348-349)

nonreciprocity principle (p. 338)

Omnibus Trade and Competitiveness Act of 1988 (p. 343)

producer subsidy equivalent (PSE) (p. 341)

public choice economics (p. 332)

Reciprocal Trade Agreements Act of 1934 (p. 336)

rent-seeking activity (p. 333)

"results-based" trade policy (p. 348)

"rules-based" trade policy (p. 348)

Smoot-Hawley Tariff (Tariff Act of 1930) (p. 336)

status quo bias (p. 333)

Strategic Impediments Initiative (SII) (p. 345)

"Super 301" clause (p. 343)

Tokyo Round of trade negotiations (p. 337)

Trade Act of 1974 (p. 337)

trade adjustment assistance (TAA) (p. 337)

Trade Expansion Act of 1962 (p. 337)

Uruguay Round of trade negotiations (p. 339)

World Trade Organization (WTO) (p. 342)

TRUE/FALSE QUESTIONS
1. The Smoot-Hawley Tariff of 1930 reduced imports, increased domestic employment, and led the U.S. out of the Great Depression.

2. Replacing bilateral negotiations with multilateral negotiations was critical to the advances in trade liberalization after WWII.

3. The across-the-board approach to negotiations was first used in the Tokyo Round of trade negotiations.

4. The trade adjustment assistance feature of the Trade Expansion Act of 1962 provided funds to help other nations match U.S. tariff adjustments.

5. Codes of behavior concerning government procurement procedures, subsidies and countervailing duties, and valuation of goods for customs purposes were established during the Tokyo Round of trade negotiations.

6. Under the fast-track procedure, Congress cannot make amendments to a negotiated agreement and must simply vote yea or nay.

7. After stalling in 1990, renewed negotiations on agricultural issues in the Uruguay Round began in 1992 as a result of a trade policy threat between the U.S. and Japan over rice exports.

8. The general principle of national treatment when applied to trade in services, means that a country imposes the same prices for foreign services as charged by domestic service providers.

9. The Strategic Impediments Initiative requires U.S. trade representatives to send Congress a designated list of nations using "unfair" impediments to trade.

10. Results-based trade policy stresses that policy should seek, through aggressive, unilateral action or threat of action, to achieve carefully specified objectives.

11. Voters that cast their vote without paying any registration fee are known as "free riders".

12. Public choice economics uses economic models to analyze government decision-making behavior.

13. Groups carrying on rent seeking activity typically expend resources in excess of the expected benefits of the policies in question.

14. Since WWII, much of U.S. foreign policy has been directed toward limiting the spread of communism.

15. Alan Deardorff (1994) indicated that the Uruguay Road would lead to an increase in global GDP from 0.7 to 1.3 percent.

FILL-IN QUESTIONS

1. A _____ trade policy is one that adheres to commonly accepted international guidelines and codes of behavior on trade.

2. A policy that treats each individual trading partner country exactly as that partner treats the home country with respect to trade is an example of the _____ approach to trade policy.

3. The organization that sponsored regular negotiations on trade liberalization between 1947 and 1993 was known as _____.

4. The _____ Round of trade negotiations was responsible for a reduction of tariffs on manufactured goods by an average of 35% in the 70 participating nations.

5. The _____ Round of trade negotiations was responsible for securing "national treatment" for services in the 117 participating nations.

6. The _____ Round of trade negotiations established a system of tariff preferences for exports from developing nations to developed nations.

7. The Uruguay Round of trade negotiations calls for _____ to replace GATT.

8. The _____ clause of the Omnibus Trade and Competitiveness Act of 1988 was designed to open foreign markets to U.S. exports.

9. The _____ system in Japan is composed of an interlocking set of firms that purchase only from each other.

10. The move from _____ negotiations with individual trading partners to _____ negotiations after WWII made a major contribution to trade liberalization.

11. The _____ holds that the decision maker who votes in such a way as to satisfy the median voter will maximize his or her reelection possibilities.

12. Groups that attempt to influence policy in their favor through the use of campaign contributions are said to be carrying on _____.

13. Activities that are not producing any good or service but merely influence the distribution of income are referred to as _____.

14. The _____ approach to trade policy is conducted taking into account the well-being of different groups in society.

15. The _____ Law gives U.S. citizens the right to sue anyone trading with investors utilizing Cuban property that was seized from U.S. citizens in 1959 when Castro came to power.

DISCUSSION QUESTIONS

1. Despite the tendency of a decision maker to focus on reelection possibilities, tariffs benefiting a small group of individuals are often imposed. Discuss the reasons this seemingly contradictory outcome may occur.

2. Outline the social objectives approach to trade policy. Discuss the problems created by a country talking the "free-trade talk" then protecting certain sectors to obtain social goals.

3. Discuss the advantages of the change from bilateral trade negotiations to multilateral negotiations after WWII. Many of the more recent trade policy actions have shown a return to bilateral negotiations. Discuss the reason for this shift and the resulting concerns.

4. The Trade Expansion Act of 1962 introduced a feature known as trade adjustment assistance (TAA). Discuss the goal of TAA and its desirability as an aspect of trade policy.

5. The Kennedy and Tokyo Rounds of trade negotiation made significant progress in reducing tariffs on manufactured good but little or no progress in agriculture. How do these sectors differ and why is progress so much more difficult in agriculture.

6. Discuss the basic concept behind the nonreciprocity principle for developing nations in the Tokyo Round agreement. What reasons are given for this preferential treatment.

7. The Uruguay Round began with a very ambitious agenda including services and trade related intellectual property restrictions. Discuss the opposition from developing nations and the compromises reached in the final agreement.

8. Explain the potential problems associated with the negotiation and ratification of trade agreements in the absence of the fast-track procedure.

9. Discuss the economic impacts of the Uruguay Round agreement. Why are these numbers relatively uncertain?

10. Discuss the intention of the "Super 301" clause to the Omnibus Trade and Competitiveness Act of 1988. Some say this act is protectionist in nature while others believe it assures open markets. Explain this confusion.

11. Discuss the structural barriers in the Japanese economy that make it difficult for American exporters. What are the estimates of the "invisible" tariff rates that result? Discuss the use of voluntary import expansions and the Strategic Impediments Initiative to help overcome these barriers.

12. Explain the differences between a "rules-based" trade policy and a "results-based" trade policy. Define managed trade and discuss its growing prominence.

13. Outline the factors that influence the degree of industry protection from the standpoint of political economy.

14. Discuss the declining role of tariffs and the growing importance of NTBs since the 1960s. Does this shift make trade liberalization easier or more difficult? Why?

CASE STUDY QUESTIONS
Refer to Case Study 1 (p. 334) Politics Puts the Squeeze on Tomato Imports

1. What evidence is provided to support the argument that the Florida tomato industry is "going down the tubes"?

2. Was the price accord reached in October 1996 a reflection of the will of the majority of the voters? Why or why not?

3. Identify and discuss the winners and losers from the tomato price accord.

4. Why are pork producers in the Midwest concerned about price supports for Florida tomato farmers?

Refer to Case Study 2 (p. 339) Sectoral Employment Impacts of Tokyo Round Trade Liberalization

1. What sectors of the economy were most impacted by the Tokyo Round tariff cuts? Given the results in Table 1, which nations were the most active in protecting these sectors?

2. Is it possible that the number of workers displaced by the Tokyo Round tariff cuts exceed these estimates? Why or why not?

3. What type of programs exist in the U.S. (and other nations as well) to aid in this movement between sectors.

Refer to Case Study 3 (p. 341) Intervention and Distortions in Agriculture

1. Using Table 2, discuss the impact of agricultural restrictions on consumers and producers in North America and the European Community.

2. What does the size of Japanese PSE and CSE relative to those of other developed nations suggest? How can this occur when nominal tariff rates on agricultural goods are lower in Japan?

3. The majority of developing nations have negative CSEs. What does this indicate about the relations between the government, agriculturists, and consumers in these nations?

4. Assume that the estimated PSEs and CSEs for Poland and the Soviet Union are correct. What does this indicate about the income transfers in a command economy?

Refer to Case Study 4 (p. 344) Restraints on U.S. Steel Imports

1. Explain how VRAs with major exporters of steel to the U.S. could adversely impact consumers and the 5 million workers in steel-using industries.

2. In 1989, Carla Hills stated that profits, employment, production, and capacity in the U.S. steel industry had all improved. Was this statement an indication that the 5 years of protection had allowed steel firms to restructure and become internationally competitive? Explain your assessment.

3. Discuss how the VRAs in place from 1984 - 1992 differed from the tariffs that began in November 1992. Which would U.S. steel producers prefer to have in place during a period of increasing demand? Why?

ANSWERS

True/False Questions
1. False
2. True
3. False
4. False
5. True
6. True
7. False
8. False
9. False
10. True
11. False
12. True
13. False
14. True
15. True

Fill-in questions
1. rules-based
2. "new reciprocity"
3. the General Agreement on Tariffs and Trade (GATT)
4. Kennedy
5. Uruguay
6. Tokyo
7. World Trade Organization (WTO)
8. Super 301
9. keiretsu
10. bilateral; multilateral
11. median-voter model
12. rent-seeking activity
13. directly unproductive activity
14. social objectives
15. Helms-Burton

CHAPTER 18
Economic Integration

SUMMARY

While most of the focus of previous chapters has been on raising or lowering barriers against all trading partners, this chapter focuses on special relationships among groups of nations. Economic integration is a process by which countries join together to create a larger economic unit with special relationships among the members. Four basic types of formal regional economic arrangements exist.

The most common form of integration is a Free Trade Area (FTA). In a FTA, members of the group remove tariffs on each others' products but maintain independence in setting policies for nonmembers. The next stage is a customs union. In a customs union, the member have no tariffs on each others' products and set common trade policies for nonmembers. The third stage is a common market. The common market adds free factor movements among member countries to the characteristics of a customs union. The final stage requires the unification of economic institutions and coordination of economic policies throughout all member countries. The movement from common market to economic union also requires adoption of a common currency.

Economic integration implies differential treatment of members and non-members. This causes changes in the pattern of trade which result in trade creation or trade diversion. The trade creation occurs when trade is shifted from a high cost domestic producer to a lower cost member producer. Trade diversion occurs when the removal of a tariff for members results in the transfer of production from a low cost world producer (still facing a tariff) to a higher cost member producer (facing no tariff). Trade creation obviously results in an increase in welfare, but trade diversion could actually result in a welfare reduction. The greater the size of the pre-integration tariffs and the closer the member cost is to the low-cost world price, the smaller the chance of a welfare loss.

Economic integration will also result in some dynamic effects on participating countries. These effects include greater competition, realization of economies of scale, greater factor mobility, and an increase in the units of bargaining power. The integration may also stimulate greater investment from members and foreign sources.

While countries are always seeking economic benefits from integration, there are certain conditions that increase the chance of overall beneficial effects. These conditions include:

> higher preunion tariffs
> lower common external tariffs
> greater elasticity of supply and demand
> the greater the number of countries
> the larger the combined economic activity
> geographic proximity.

The largest and best known integration unit is the European Union. From its origin with six countries in 1951, this unit has progressed from free trade area to customs union on to common market. The membership has grown to fifteen nations and there are efforts to complete the transition to an economic union. While growth was strong during the early stages of integration, the European Union is now faced with slower growth, relatively high unemployment, and other countries wanting to join the integration unit.

The opposite case is present in Central/Eastern Europe and the Former Soviet Union. The integration of these nations through the Council for Mutual Economic Assistance (CMEA) has ended. The CMEA nation had extremely high rates of trade with other members and the recent "disintegration" has led to greater trade with the rest of the world. While the transition to market economies will lead to more integration with the rest of the world, the process of transition is difficult and entails some very high costs. Success has been more likely when liberalization policies have been consistent and property rights are clearly defined.

The United States has also been involved in the process of economic integration. On January 1, 1989, the Canada - US Free Trade Agreement linked the U.S. to its largest trading partner. This agreement was followed by the negotiation of the North American Free Trade Agreement linking Canada, the U.S., and Mexico. While NAFTA proved to be very controversial it was approved in late 1993 and took effect on January 1, 1994. NAFTA will eliminate tariffs among the three member nations over a fifteen year period and drop barriers to the movement of financial services and capital.

A variety of other economic integration efforts have been established in the 1990's. MERCOSUR is an attempt by Argentina, brazil, Paraguay, and Uruguay to create a customs union. Discussions have been held to initiate a Free Trade Area for the Americas (FTAA) that would go beyond NAFTA and MERCOSUR. Free trade for the eighteen nations bordering the Pacific is the goal of the Asia Pacific Economic Cooperation Forum (APEC).

DEFINE THE FOLLOWING KEY TERMS
Asia Pacific Economic Cooperation Forum (APEC) (p. 375)

Canada-U.S. Free Trade Agreement (p. 370)

common external tariff (p. 355)

common market (p. 355)

customs union (p. 355)

dynamic effects of economic integration (p. 361)

EC92 (p. 366)

economic union (p. 355)

European Community (EC) (p. 355)

European Free Trade Association (EFTA) (p. 355)

European Union (p. 355)

"Eurosclerosis" (p. 365)

ex post income elasticity of import demand (p. 360)

Free Trade Area for the Americas (FTAA) (p. 374)

free trade area (p. 353)

maquiladora program (p. 372)

MERCOSUR (p. 374)

monetary union (p. 355)

North American Free Trade Agreement (NAFTA) (p. 370-371)

rules of origin (p. 355)

second best (p. 356)

Single European Act (p. 365)

static effects of economic integration (p. 356)

trade creation (p. 356)

trade diversion (p. 356)

transition economies (p. 369)

transshipment (p. 355)

TRUE/FALSE QUESTIONS

1. Economic integration represents a partial movement to free trade in a context where countries accord differential treatment to their trading partners.

2. Trade diversion takes place whenever there is a shift in product origin from a member producer to a lower cost producer who is outside the integration unit.

3. When a customs union involves some trade diversion, the result is necessarily a reduction in welfare for the nation and possibly the entire unit.

4. If transportation costs are considered, static and dynamic gains are more likely the closer the member countries geographically.

5. Two of the major reasons that economic integration often fails are the issue of national sovereignty and the realization of substantial economies of scale.

6. The European Union reached the stage of full economic union as a result of the Single European Act on December 31, 1992.

7. The formation of the European Community began with the Treaty of France being signed by Belgium, France, Great Britain, West Germany, Luxembourg, and the Netherlands.

8. Low growth rates, slow rates of modernization, and generally poor economic performance were important factors in the breakup of the USSR.

9. By international standards, the percent of total trade of Central/Eastern European nations with other members of the CMEA was high in the 1980s.

10. The North American Free Trade Agreement eliminates all tariff barriers between the U.S., Canada, and Mexico over a five year period.

FILL-IN QUESTIONS

1. A form of economic integration in which tariff barriers are removed between members, a common external trade policy is adopted, and all barriers to factor movements among members are removed is known as a _____.

2. A _____ is a form of economic integration in which tariff barriers are removed between members and a common external trade policy is adopted.

3. A _____ is a form of economic integration that implies the unification of economic institutions and the coordination of economic policies (including a common currency).

4. A form of economic integration in which all members of the group remove tariffs on each others products while maintaining independence in establishing trade policies with nonmembers is known as a _____.

5. When economic integration leads to a shift in product origin from a domestic producer whose resource costs are higher to a member producer whose resource costs are lower is a case of _____.

6. The results of economic integration are more likely to be positive the _____ the level of preunion tariffs and the _____ the common external barriers.

7. The results of economic integration will more likely be positive the more _____ supply and demand in the member countries.

8. The positive effects of an economic integration will be larger the _____ the number of participating countries and the _____ the economic size of the group.

9. The term _____ is used to refer to relatively and absolutely low growth rates in the EC and the high European unemployment rates.

10. An attempt to develop and adopt concrete steps to achieve free trade and investment in the Asia/Pacific area by the year 2020 is known as _____.

DISCUSSION QUESTIONS

1. Discuss the development of the European Union in terms of the four stages of economic integration.

2. Define trade creation and trade diversion. Discuss the impacts of relative costs of production, pre-integration tariff levels, and elasticities of supply and demand on the welfare effect of integration being positive.

3. Choose six nations and use the conditions under which economic integration is likely to have beneficial overall effects to create a successful and an unsuccessful unit. Explain the success (or failure) in each unit.

4. The 1985 European Commission's "White Paper" outlined some of the difficulties experienced in the ECs transition to a common market. Discuss the hindrances and restrictions along with the progress that has been made in removing them. Outline the problems facing the European Union in the future.

5. Discuss the relatively closed nature of CMEA trade and the problems being experienced by former members in their attempts at privatization and greater integration into the world economy.

6. Explain why NAFTA was much more hotly debated than the Canada-US Free Trade Agreement. Discuss the expected sectoral impacts in terms of US "export winners" and "import losers".

7. In recent years, Chile has been the most active nation in the Western hemisphere in establishing special trade agreements. Discuss these agreements and the changes in the Chilean economy that led to this wave of trade agreements.

PROBLEMS

1. Given the following information and assuming no transportation costs, answer the following questions about prices and quantities of good 1 consumed in Country A.

	Price	Pre-integration Quantity	Post-integration Quantity
Country A	$2.00	150	120
Country B	$1.50	50	180

    Prior to integration Country A places a 20% tariff on its imports from Country B. After integration the tariffs are removed on imports from Country B.

    a. What is the total pre-integration consumption of good 1 in country A?

    b. What price is paid by the consumers in Country A before integration?

    c. What price is paid by the consumers in Country A after integration?

    d. What is the total consumption of good 1 in Country A after integration?

    e. How much production was switched from Country A to Country B as a result of the integration?

    f. Calculate the net welfare gain from this trade creation.

    g. How much production was switched from Country A to Country B as a result of the integration?

    h. Calculate the consumer welfare gain from additional consumption.

    i. Calculate the net welfare gain for Country A.

2. Given the following 3 country case (A,B,C) with one good (good 1) and no transportation costs:

	Price	Pre-integration Quantity	Post-integration Quantity
Country A	$2.00	80	70
Country B	$1.40	0	80
Country C	$1.00	60	0

Prior to integration Country A places a 50% tariff on imports of good 1. As a result of economic integration between countries A and B all tariffs are removed on imports from Country B. Imports from Country C still face the 50% tariff.

a. What is the total pre-integration consumption of good 1 in Country A?

b. What is the pre-integration price of good 1 imported from Country B?

c. What is the pre-integration price of good 1 imported from Country C?

d. What is the total consumption of good 1 in Country A after integration?

e. What is the post-integration price of good 1 imported from Country B?

f. What is the post-integration price of good 1 imported from Country C?

g. How much production was switched from Country A to Country B as a result of the integration?

h. Calculate the net welfare gain from this trade creation.

i. How much did consumption increase as a result of the economic integration?

j. Calculate the net welfare gain from additional consumption.

k. How much trade was diverted from Country C to Country B as a result of the integration?

l. Calculate the value of the trade diversion.

m. Calculate the net effect of the integration between countries A and B.

CASE STUDY QUESTIONS
Refer to Case Study 1 (p. 354) Economic Integration Units

1. Discuss the geographic nature of the integration units in Table 1. What are the geographic impacts on the chance of a successful integration unit?

2. In addition to geography, what factors seem to have influenced the integration units in Table 1? Explain.

3. The table contains a large number of common markets relative to economic unions. Discuss the potential difficulties associated with the economic union level of integration.

Refer to Case Study 2 (p. 360) Trade Creation and Trade Diversion in the European Community

1. In Table 2, the intra-area imports are seen as a measure of trade creation. Discuss this increase in imports in terms of potential gains by domestic producers.

2. In Table 2, the extra-area imports are seen as a measure of trade diversion. Discuss this change in imports from the standpoint of the domestic producer, domestic consumer, and world efficiency.

3. While the increase in Total Imports (in Table 2) is seen as a measure of trade creation, discuss the dynamic effects of integration that could lead to even greater benefits.

Refer to Case Study 3 (p. 363) The East African Community

1. Did the terms of the East African Common Market fit the definition of a common market? Why or why not?

2. What historical characteristics made these three nations seem to be a very good fit for integration?

3. Sovereignty and the distribution of the benefits are the two most common problems for an integration unit. Discuss their role in the breakup of the East African Community.

Refer to Case Study 4 (p. 373) The Mexican Maquiladoras

1. What aspects of the maquiladoras are attractive to U.S. firms?

2. What aspects of the maquiladora process are attractive to Mexico?

3. Discuss the presence of Japanese and European firms in Mexico in terms of transshipment. Will transshipment continue to be a strategy with NAFTA? What factors are involved in the success of that strategy?

4. Explain why a U.S. firm may have fewer difficulties working through a maquila than they experience in a normal foreign investment. Be sure to consider the cultural issues in your answer.

ANSWERS

<u>True/False Questions</u>
1. True
2. False
3. False
4. True
5. False
6. False
7. False
8. True
9. True
10. False

<u>Fill-in questions</u>
1. common market
2. customs union
3. economic union
4. free trade area
5. trade creation
6. higher; lower
7. elastic
8. greater; larger
9. Eurosclerosis
10. the Asia Pacific Economic Cooperation Forum

<u>Problems</u>
1.   a. 200 units
   b. $1.50 + (1.50 x 2) = 1.50 + .30 = $1.80
   c. $1.50
   d. 300 units
   e. 150 - 120 = 30 units switched to the lower cost producer
   f. 1/2 (30)($.30) = 1/2 ($9) = $4.50
   g. 100 units
   h. 1/2 (100)($.30) = 50($.3) = $15.00
   i. $4.50 + $15.00 = $19.50

2.   a. 140 units
   b. $2.10
   c. $1.50
   d. 150 units
   e. $1.40
   f. $1.50
   g. 80 - 70 = 10 units
   h. 1/2 (10) ($.10) = $.50

i. 10 units
j. 1/2 (10) ($.10) = $.50
k. 60 units
l. (60) (.10) = $6.00
m. $.50 + $.50 - $6.00 = -$5.00 (a loss of five dollars)

CHAPTER 19
International Trade and the Developing Countries

SUMMARY

The developing nations of the world account for three-quarters of the world's population but only one-quarter of production and income. There are serious concerns that the characteristics and conditions of these nations differ so far from the theoretical ideals discussed in earlier chapters that adherence to free trade may not increase welfare and promote development.

The nations of the developing world are characterized by low per-capita income, high inflation, predominately rural populations, and low life expectancy. To the extent that these nations are involved in the world trading system, they tend to export primary products and import manufactured products. Recent trends suggest increases in export activity and reductions in imports in attempt to control balance of payment problems.

While traditional trade theories would suggest gains from concentrating production in their comparative advantage goods, developing nations may not have the flexibility and responsiveness to realize the gains. These nations tend to have comparative advantages in labor-intensive goods and international demand may not justify increased production of these products. Low income and price elasticities of demand, increased dependence of industrialized nations and undesirable terms of trade effects are major concerns for exporters of primary products.

Significant differences in the characteristics of developing nations suggest that the static effects of the theoretical model may not be realized. The differences in LDC characteristics include:

>   imperfect competition
>   unemployment
>   factor market imperfections
>   lack of impact of primary products on other sectors
>   differences in scale characteristics
>   less developed government policies.

Many argue that the differences in the goods traded result in a greater share of trade-related benefits going to developed countries. The two issues most closely related to this distributional imbalance are export instability and long run terms of trade deterioration. Export instability refers to the greater fluctuation of prices and earnings associated with primary products. The instability in export prices and earnings is usually attributed to inelastic supply and demand of primary products and a lack of diversification in production.

The problem of long run terms of trade deterioration is in the transfer of income from developing nations to developed nations over time. While there is a disagreement over the existence of a transfer, the causes usually include differences in income elasticity of demand between primary products and manufactured goods, differences in market power, technological advances, and pricing practices of multinational corporations.

In light of the concerns associated with the impact of trade in developing countries, several policies have been used to stabilize prices or improve terms of trade. A variety of trade policies have been used to stabilize prices or export earnings. These policies include international buffer stock agreements, international export quota agreements, and compensatory financing. None of these policies have been judged very successful in practice and concerns exist as to the feasibility and desirability for developing nations.

The concerns associated with long run deterioration in the terms of trade are often addressed through export diversification to include more manufactured goods, the formation of export cartels, the use of import and export restrictions and economic integration. The attempts to find the appropriate trade policy for developing nations often center on the focus of the trade strategy.

The advocates of an inward-looking strategy attempt to withdraw from full participation in the world economy. A major emphasis is on import substitution to produce domestically what has previously been imported. This strategy is very protectionist. An outward-looking strategy emphasizes international trade. The policy focuses on production according to comparative advantages and exposing firms to the discipline of free international competition. The extreme version uses subsidies and other policies for export promotion.

Examinations of comparative performances of countries under different trade policies suggest that an outward-looking policy may enhance economic performance. The experience of the East Asian countries have demonstrated the viability of trade policies that promote industrialization and the ability of developing nations to move beyond reliance on primary commodities. In general, all policies have their difficulties and recommendations must be decided on a case by case basis.

DEFINE THE FOLLOWING KEY TERMS
commodity concentration (p. 384)

compensatory financing (p. 390)

differing income elasticities of demand for primary products and manufactured goods (p. 387)

export cartel (p. 394)

export diversification into manufactured goods (p. 394)

export instability (p. 383)

export promotion (p. 396)

"get prices right" (p. 396)

high degree of openness (p. 383)

import substitution (p. 396)

international buffer stock agreement (p. 390)

international export quota agreement (p. 390)

intrafirm trade (p. 388)

inward-looking strategy (p. 396)

long-run deterioration in the terms of trade (p. 385)

moderately-inward-oriented economy (p. 396)

moderately-outward-oriented economy (p. 396)

outward-looking strategy (p. 396)

Prebisch-Singer hypothesis (p. 385)

repatriation of earnings (p. 388)

strongly-inward-oriented economy (p. 396)

strongly-outward-oriented economy (p. 396)

unequal market power in product and factor markets (p. 387)

vent for surplus (p. 381)

TRUE/FALSE QUESTIONS
1. While the title developing nations refers to over 120 countries, this group is very homogeneous in income, industrial structure, and participation in international trade.

2. The degree of participation in international trade (measured by export growth) by low-income countries decreased in the 1990-94 period as compared to the 1980-90 period.

3. Because the economic systems of the developing countries tend to be somewhat unresponsive to changing price incentives, at least in the short run, factors of production may not move easily to expanding low-cost sectors.

4. The "vent for surplus" concept suggests that developing countries are a potential market for the surplus products of developed nations.

5. The dynamic effects of trade on development include the realization of economies of scale, increased dissemination of technology, and exposure to new and different products.

6. The relatively high degree of openness of many developing countries refers to their high ratio of foreign trade to gross domestic product.

7. The hypothesis that there has been a long run tendency for commodity concentration to increase in developing countries is known as the Prebisch-Singer hypothesis.

8. If MNCs use a transfer pricing strategy to avoid taxes, recorded taxes will be higher in a low-tax and easy repatriation industrialized country and lower in the high tax, difficult repatriation developing country.

9. In the case of international commodity agreements, if supply curve shifts cause the instability the agreements can reduce the level of export earnings and the producer welfare in the LDC.

10. Import substitution policies often result in foreign exchange shortages and capital intensive production processes that displace labor.

FILL-IN QUESTIONS

1. The dynamic effects of trade on development arise from increased _____ resulting from changes in the economic environment and increased dissemination of _____ into the developing country.

2. Possible negative effects of trade on development arise from _____ in developing countries generally resulting in private costs and benefits being different from social costs and benefits.

3. Since economy-wide production linkages may vary between commodities, the commodities whose export growth have a relatively large impact on growth and development of the entire economy are known as _____.

4. LDCs in which one or two goods constitute a majority of total export earnings are said to have a high degree of _____.

5. The problem of _____ refers to the allegation that, over a span of several decades, there has been a persistent tendency for commodity terms of trade to fall for developing countries.

6. Empirical evidence on differing income elasticities of demand suggest that the income elasticity of demand is usually greater than one of _____ and less than one for _____.

7. For MNC sending products between subsidiaries, _____ are largely arbitrary because the goods do not pass through organized markets, and the recorded prices are merely bookkeeping entries for the firm.

8. In an international buffer stock agreement, if the world price falls below the floor price, the agency will _____ the product. On the other hand, if the world price is above the ceiling, the agency will _____ the product to maintain price stability.

9. The formation of an _____ may successfully combat long run terms of trade deterioration if all exporting countries are part of the process, no strong substitutes exist, and cheating can be prevented.

10. An _____ trade strategy emphasizes participation in international trade by encouraging the allocation of resources without price distortions.

DISCUSSION QUESTIONS

1. Discuss the conditions in developing countries that differ significantly from the theoretical world of the trade models. Explain how these differences may impact the predicted static gains from trade.

2. The traditional trade models suggest that most developing nations should specialize in and export labor-intensive products. Many observers question the desirability of growth in traditional goods if it comes at the expense of modern manufacturing. Explain the concerns of these observers.

3. A major concern for many developing nations is export instability. Discuss the potential causes and difficulties associated with the resulting uncertainty.

4. The belief that the international economy is transferring real income from LDCs to ICs has been widely debated. Discuss the origin of the hypothesis and the results of attempts to empirically verify the trend.

5. Explain the four reasons that have been offered for the alleged long-run terms of trade decline for developing countries.

6. International buffer stock agreements and international export quota agreements have been offered as policies to stabilize prices and export earnings. Discuss the difficulties associated with effectively implementing these plans over a sustained period of time.

7. Explain the general policy measures that have been suggested to alleviate the TOT deterioration of LDCs and provide an example of each.

8. One reaction to the trade problems of developing countries is to withdraw from participation in the world economy. Discuss the major aspects of an import substitution program and the characteristics of a nation classified as inward-oriented by the World Development Report 1987.

9. Discuss the major aspects of export promotion strategy and the characteristics of a nation classified as outward-oriented by the World Development Report 1987.

10. "The figures suggest that the economic performance of the outward-oriented economies has been superior to that of the inward-oriented economies in almost all respects." Given this outcome, why have economists been reluctant to wholeheartedly embrace the outward-oriented policy for all developing nations?

PROBLEMS

1. Given the information in Table 1 on page 378, answer the following questions:
   a. Which category experienced the highest annual per-capita GDP growth?

   b. Which category experienced the greatest annual inflation?

   c. Which category has more than half of the population living in rural areas?

   d. What type of relationship exists between the infant mortality rate and years of life expectancy at birth?

   e. What type of relationship exists between income category and percentage of the labor force in agriculture?

2. Given the export demand and supply curves in Figure 1 on page 384, answer the following questions:
   a. Name two changes that result in an increase in the price of the export good.

   b. Name two changes that result in a decrease in the price of the export good.

   c. In panel a, as the supply curve becomes relatively more inelastic the instability of prices (increases/decreases).

   d. In panel b, as the demand curve becomes more inelastic the instability of prices (increases/decreases).

   e. Give some reasons that the supply and demand of primary products tend to be relatively inelastic.

3. Given the Buffer Stock diagrams in Figure 2 on page 392, answer the following questions.

   a. In panel a, if D_1 represents the demand in period 1 and P_S is the stabilized price, will the agency be forced to buy or sell output to maintain the stabilized price?

   b. Identify the following in panel a:
      (1) with demand D_1, quantity demanded and quantity supplied at price P_S.

      (2) with demand D_2, quantity demanded and quantity supplied at price P_S.

(3) export earnings in both periods with the buffer stock

(4) with demand at D_1, quantity demanded and quantity supplied without the buffer stock

(5) export earnings with demand at D_1 without the buffer stock

(6) with demand at D_2, quantity demanded and quantity supplied without the buffer stock

(7) export earnings with demand at D_2 without the buffer stock

c. If the instability of the prices is related to demand fluctuations (panel a), the operation of the buffer stock (enhances/reduces) the consumer surplus in the buying countries and (enhances/reduces) the producer surplus of the LDC producers.

d. If the instability of the prices is related to supply fluctuations (panel b), the operation of the buffer stock (enhances/reduces) the consumer surplus in the buying countries and (enhances/reduces) the producer surplus of the LDC producers.

CASE STUDY QUESTIONS
Refer to Case Study 1 (p. 397) Price Distortions in Pakistani Agriculture

1. Government procurement is a means to stabilize export prices. Is the Pakistani government achieving its objective? What is the cost of the program to the Pakistani farmer?

2. Is the current Pakistani agricultural export policy developing incentives that support its comparative advantages? Explain.

3. If the adoption of an export-oriented strategy included an emphasis on "getting the prices right", what adjustments need to be made. How would these adjustments impact production?

ANSWERS

True/False Questions
1. False
2. False
3. True
4. False
5. True
6. True
7. False
8. True
9. False
10. True

Fill-in questions
1. investment; technology
2. market imperfections
3. growth poles

4. commodity concentration
5. long run deterioration in the terms of trade
6. manufactured goods; primary products
7. intrafirm trade prices
8. buy; sell
9. export cartel
10. outward looking

Problems
1.
   a. low income
   b. upper-middle income
   c. low income
   d. inverse (negative) as the infant mortality rate declines, life expectancy rises
   e. inverse (negative) as income rises the percentage of labor force in agriculture falls

2.
   a. increase in demand; decrease in supply
   b. decrease in demand; increase in supply
   c. increases
   d. increases
   e. <u>demand</u> tends to be inelastic because the goods are inputs so demand is derived from demand for the final good or the goods are food products which historically face low elasticities.
   <u>supply</u> tends to be inelastic because the goods have a fixed production cycle (harvesting time) and producers have little ability to adjust production in the short run.

3.
   a. excess supply means the agency must buy
   b.
   (1) quantity demanded = OQ_4 quantity supplied = OQ_3
   (2) quantity demanded = OQ_5 quantity supplied = OQ_3
   (3) OP_sBQ_3
   (4) quantity demanded = OQ_1 quantity supplied = OQ_1
   (5) $OP_1E_1Q_1$
   (6) quantity demanded = OQ_2 quantity supplied = OQ_2
   (7) $OP_2E_2Q_2$
   c. enhances; reduces
   d. reduces; enhances

CHAPTER 20
The Balance of Payments Accounts

SUMMARY

A country's balance of payments statement is a reflection of that nations' activity with the rest of the world during a given year. The transactions recorded move well beyond goods and services to include international financial transactions by individuals, corporations, financial institutions, and governments. The examinations of balance of payments accounts over the last 20 years provides evidence of the rapid growth of trade and the increasing interdependence of the world financial markets.

As a general working rule, transactions that give rise to payments inward to a home country are credit items (+) in the balance of payments account. Transactions that give rise to payments outward from the home country are recorded as debit items (-) in the balance of payments account. The debit and credit items are grouped into four major categories:

> Category I   Current Account
> Category II   Direct Investment and long-term capital flows
> Category III Short-term non-official capital flows
> Category IV Changes in reserve assets of official monetary authorities.

All transactions involve two entries (one credit and one debit) under the system of double entry bookkeeping.

All of a nation's transactions during a given year are recorded and used to assemble the nation's balance of payments statement. The top of the statement focuses on exports and imports of goods. The difference (X-M) yields the balance of trade or merchandise trade balance. This stage of the process is often reported as a merchandise trade surplus or deficit. The next stage considers the imports and exports of services. The net balance on services is combined with the merchandise trade balance to provide the balance on goods and services.

The next step is the addition of investment income (income investment receipts from abroad - investment income payments abroad) to obtain the balance of goods, services, and investment income. The addition of net unilateral transfers completes category I and provides the current account balance. The consideration of the long term capital account is the focus of category II. Net increase in foreign long-term assets in the country minus the net increase in long-term assets abroad is added to the current account balance to obtain the basic balance. The basic balance is considered the best reflection of long-term forces in the economy of a country.

Category III adds short term private assets. The net increase in foreign short-term assets in the country minus the net increase in short-term assets abroad is added to the basic balance to provide the official reserve transactions balance. The official reserve transactions balance is also known as the overall balance. Category IV reflects the government activity necessary to "settle" the net balance of the previous transactions. These transactions that occur because of other activity in the balance of payments are known as accommodating items in the balance of payments. The net result of all entries is a balance of $0.

The actual balance of payments for the U.S. and other nations do not quite conform to the four categories discussed. The short-term and long-term assets tend to be combined in the reporting. Data on financing and capital flows are gathered from financial institutions while goods and services data are recorded by customs. The timing and accuracy of the two sources do not always coincide and a statistical discrepancy entry is necessary to bring the final balance to $0.

The final statement is concerned with the stock of foreign capital and is known as the international investment position of a country. The international investment position shows the cumulative size of a country's foreign assets and liabilities at a given point in time. By 1987, the rapid inflow of capital into the U.S. created the case where foreign assets in the U.S. exceeded U.S. assets abroad. The U.S. moved in 1987 from a position of net creditor country to be a net debtor country. In 1995, the U.S. held the position as the world's largest net debtor with an international investment position of -$814 billion.

DEFINE THE FOLLOWING KEY TERMS
accommodating items in the balance of payments (p. 413)

autonomous items in the balance of payments (p. 413)

balance of payments accounts (p. 403)

balance of trade or merchandise trade balance (p. 409)

balance of trade deficit or merchandise trade deficit (p. 409-410)

balance of trade surplus or merchandise trade surplus (p. 409)

balance on current account and long-term capital or basic balance (p. 412) balance on goods and services (p. 410)

balance on goods, services, and investment income (p. 411)

capital account balance (p. 413)

credit items in the balance of payments accounts (p. 406)

current account balance or balance on current account (p. 411)

debit items in the balance of payments accounts (p. 406)

double-entry bookkeeping (p. 407)

favorable trade balance (p. 410)

international investment position of a country or international indebtedness position of a country (p. 417)

net creditor country (p. 417)

net debtor country (p. 417)

official reserve transactions balance or overall balance (p. 413)

statistical discrepancy or net errors and omissions (p. 417)

unfavorable trade balance (p. 410)

TRUE/FALSE QUESTIONS

1. During the period from 1973 to 1996, the value of world exports grew from $582 billion to $5100 billion.

2. Gold has been replaced by U.S. dollars, Japanese Yen, and German deutsche marks as the most widely held international reserve asset.

3. Credit items in the balance of payments accounts include imports, investments made in foreign countries by domestic nationals, and payments of interest and dividends by the home country on earlier investments made in it by foreign nationals.

4. A nation's exports of goods and services are recorded as part of a nation's current account.

5. Payments for U.S. imports made by transferring funds from the buyer's checking account to the foreign firms bank account in a U.S. bank would be categorized as an increase in foreign short-term private assets in the U.S.

6. When the imports of goods exceed the exports of goods, the result is referred to as a merchandise trade surplus.

7. When net investment income is added to the balance on goods and services, the result is known as the basic balance or balance on current account and long term capital.

8. Government transactions that occur because of other activity in the balance of payments are known as autonomous items in the balance of payments.

9. A country's capital account in its balance of payments represents a flow of capital while the international investment position of a country is a stock of capital at a point in time.

10. Since 1987, the U.S. has enjoyed the status as a net creditor country.

FILL-IN QUESTIONS

1. Transactions that give rise to payments inward to the home country are recorded as _____ in the balance of payments account.

2. The principle of _____ means that any transaction involves the recording of the monetary amount twice - once as a debit and once as a credit.

3. In the balance of payments account exports of goods minus imports of goods is known as the _____.

4. The balance on goods and services plus (investment income receipts from abroad minus investment income payments abroad) is known as the _____.

5. The balance on current account adds _____ to the balance on goods, service, and investment income.

6. In the basic macroeconomic identity $Y=C+I+G+(X-M)$, the $(X-M)$ actually refers to the _____ balance from the balance of payments account.

7. The basic balance is also known as the balance on current account and _____.

8. The addition of short-term private capital flows to the basic balance results in the _____.

9. An examination of the international investment position of the U.S. show that the U.S. was a _____ country until 1987 and has been a _____ country since 1987.

10. The sum of categories II - IV in the balance of payments account is known as the _____.

DISCUSSION QUESTIONS

1. Discuss the difference between credit and debit items in the balance of payments accounts. Give three examples of each.

2. The basic balance or balance on current account and long-term capital reflects the basic long-term forces in the economy of a country. Explain why.

3. The final entry in the U.S. balance of payments account (Table 6) is a measure of statistical discrepancy. Discuss some of the reasons this term is necessary to balance the accounts.

4. Discuss the differences between the entries recorded in the capital account and those in the current account.

5. Discuss the advantages and disadvantages of the U.S.'s position as a net debtor country.

6. Explain the relationship between a nation's international investment position and its capital account in the balance of payments.

PROBLEMS

1. Take the following international transactions and enter them into the debit and credit table below:

   a. Consumers in Country A import $7000 of goods and payment is made by transferring $7000 to country B's bank account in country A.

   b. A resident of country A buys a $5000 long-term bond issued by a company in country B and the payment is deposited by the country B firm in its country A bank account.

   c. Residents of country A receive $2000 of services from country B citizens as a gift.

   d. A country B firm pays $4000 in dividends to country A investors and payment is made by the country B firm writing a $4000 check on its country A bank account.

   e. A country B firm invests $10,000 in new equipment in its country A plant and pays with a $10,000 check on its country A bank account.

International Transactions Country A

Debits (-)	Credits

2. Take the international transactions from the table in Problem 1 and develop a balance of payments account for country A.

Balance of Payments Summary Statement, Country A

3. Given the following:

Total U.S. assets abroad - $350 billion
Total foreign assets in the U.S. - $620 billion

Find the Net International Investment Position of the U.S.

CASE STUDY QUESTIONS

Refer to Case Study 1 (p. 418) Japan's Trade and Current Account Surpluses

1. In figure 1, the Japanese current account balance is continually below the trade balance. Explain the cause of this divergence. Does this provide any opportunities for the U.S.?

2. Japan's overall balance (official transactions balance) has averaged only +4.2 billion annually. What does this say about capital activity in the Japanese economy?

3. If Japan imports more goods from the U.S. than any other nation is the U.S. claim of the "closed" nature of the Japanese economy justified?

4. What are the characteristics of the nations that run trade surpluses with Japan? What sectors provide opportunities for the U.S. to improve its trade balance with Japan?

Refer to Case Study 2 (p. 420) Trends in the U.S. International Investment Position

1. What does the decline in the U.S. net international investment position say about U.S. capital accounts? What does this mean for the U.S. current account? Explain this relationship.

2. Discuss some factors related to the net capital inflow since 1980.

3. How does the net direct investment position differ from the net international investment position? What do the differences between these two measures indicate about the nature of the capital inflow?

4. Discuss the differences between the net debtor status in an international investment position and the net debtor position in terms of the national debt.

ANSWERS

True/False Questions
1. True
2. True
3. False
4. True
5. True
6. False
7. False
8. False
9. True
10. False

Fill-in questions
1. credit items
2. double entry bookkeeping
3. balance of trade or merchandise trade balance
4. balance on goods, services, and investment income
5. net unilateral transfers (unilateral transfers received minus unilateral transfers made)
6. current account
7. long term capital
8. official reserves transactions balance or overall balance
9. net creditor, net debtor
10. capital account balance

Problems
1.

International Transactions Country A

	Debits (-)	Credits
a.	imports of goods -7000	Increase in foreign short-term assets in country A +7000
b.	increase in long-term assets abroad -5000	increase in foreign short-term assets in country A +5000
c.	imports of services -2000	unilateral transfer made +2000
d.	decrease in foreign short-term assets in Country A -4000	investment income receipts +4000
e.	decrease in foreign short-term assets in Country A -10,000	increase in foreign long-term assets in country A +10,000

2. Balance of Payments Summary Statement, Country A

I.

Exports of goods	0
Imports of goods	-7,000
Balance of trade	-7,000
Export of services	0
Import of services	-2,000
Balance on goods and services	-9,000
Investment income receipts from abroad	+4,000
Investment income payments abroad	0
Balance on goods, services, and investment income	-5,000
Unilateral transfers received	+2,000
Unilateral transfers made	0
Balance on current account	-3,000

II.

Net increase in foreign long term assets in country A	+10,000
Net increase in long-term assets abroad	-5,000
Basic balance	+2,000

III.

Net increase in foreign short term private assets in country A (+7000 + 5000 - 4000 - 10,000) = -2000	2,000
Net increase in short-term private assets abroad	0
Official reserve transactions balance	0

IV.

Net increase in short term official assets in country A	0
Net increase in official reserve assets or official assets abroad	0
	$ 0

3. $350 - $620 = -270 billion

CHAPTER 21
The Foreign Exchange Market

SUMMARY

One of the major differences between international transactions and trade within a nation is the need to convert values from one currency to another. To facilitate these conversions, the foreign exchange market handles the exchange of foreign currencies. In this market, the price of one currency in terms of another is known as the foreign exchange rate.

There are a variety of reasons that individuals choose to participate in the foreign exchange market. On the demand side, individuals demand foreign exchange to buy imports, to invest abroad, to acquire foreign assets, or for speculation. On the supply side, foreign currency supply to the home country results from foreign purchases of exports, foreign purchases of home assets, and foreign speculation.

The intersection of the supply and demand for foreign currency curves determines the exchange rate and the equilibrium quantity of foreign currency. An increase in the exchange rate means that it takes more units of the home currency to obtain a unit of the foreign currency. This is referred to as home currency depreciation or foreign currency appreciation. A decrease in the home currency price of foreign currency is referred to as home currency appreciation or foreign currency depreciation.

The foreign exchange market is actually divided into different markets for different time frames. The daily or current market is referred to as the spot market. Although foreign exchange is traded in a variety of locations worldwide, arbitrage prevents persistent differences in exchange rates across locations. While the spot exchange rate is critical for international currency exchanges, other exchange rates are used to measure the strength of a nation's currency when there are multiple trading partners. The effective exchange rate (EER) is a trade weighted average relative strength of a given currency. The real exchange rate (RER) includes the impact of changing relative prices between two nations. The real effective exchange rate (REER) is a trade weighted average of the relative strength of a currency using real instead of nominal exchange rates. The purchasing power parity (PPP) approach focuses on the equilibrium exchange rate that would lead to the current account being in balance.

Many foreign exchange transactions are set with a delivery date beyond the value date (more than two days in the future). These transactions take place in the forward market. By contracting for delivery of foreign exchange at some time in the future, the trader locks in the exchange at the forward exchange rate. The forward market can be used to hedge against changes in the spot rate or to speculate by taking long or short positions. The buying or selling of foreign currency in the future can also take place through the use of futures contracts or foreign currency options.

While there are three separate markets (spot, forward, and futures/options), exchange rates and the interest rates in various countries are determined simultaneously. These all come together in an investor's process of deciding whether to invest in the home country or abroad. The three critical elements are:

(1) the domestic interest rate
(2) the foreign interest rate
(3) any expected changes in the exchange rate.

The investor must move beyond a comparison of the two interest rates to consider expected appreciation or depreciation of the foreign currency and the risk premium.

The investor does not have to assume all the risk associated with changes in the exchange rate. The investor can take a covered investment position by hedging in the forward market. In equilibrium, any difference in interest rates between the two financial markets should be offset by the premium associated with the use of the forward market. The link between the spot market, forward markets, and the money markets that generates this equilibrium is covered interest arbitrage. The movement of funds from one nation to another as a result of interest rate differentials and forward market premiums are predicted through the use of the covered interest arbitrage parity conditions.

A variety of real world factors make it difficult to actually observe the adjustment process in foreign exchange markets. Transaction costs and multiple interest rates in a nation hamper the adjustment process. Additional impediments include government policies and institutional imperfections. The determination of exchange rates and potential volatility are discussed in future chapters.

DEFINE THE FOLLOWING KEY TERMS
absolute purchasing power parity (p. 434)

arbitrage (p. 429)

at discount (p. 444)

at premium (p. 444)

covered interest arbitrage (p. 444)

covered interest arbitrage parity (p. 445)

cross-rate equality (p. 430)

effective exchange rate (p.431)

efficient foreign exchange market (p. 447)

expected spot rate (p. 442)

expected percentage appreciation of the foreign currency (p. 442)

foreign currency option (p. 440)

foreign exchange market (p. 425)

foreign exchange rate (p. 425)

forward exchange rate (p. 438)

futures contract (p. 439)

hedging (p. 426)

home currency appreciation (or foreign currency depreciation) (p. 427)

home currency depreciation (or foreign currency appreciation) (p. 427)

interbank market (p. 429)

law of one price (p. 434)

long position (p. 439)

purchasing power parity (p. 434)

real effective exchange rate (p. 432)

real exchange rate (p. 432)

relative purchasing power parity (p. 434)

retail spread or retail trading margin (p. 437)

risk premium (p. 443)

short position (p. 439)

speculation (p. 426)

spot market (p. 429)

triangular arbitrage (p. 430)

uncovered interest parity (p. 443)

uncovered or open position (p. 437)

value date (p. 437)

TRUE/FALSE QUESTIONS

1. An importer contracts with a bank to acquire foreign currency on a date two months in the future in the spot market.

2. The most common exchange of currencies takes place two business days after the exchange contract has been struck in the forward market.

3. A futures contract is an agreement to buy or sell a specified quantity of foreign currency for delivery at a future point in time at a given exchange rate through the Chicago Mercantile Exchange.

4. Acquiring a currency today at a low price in hopes of selling it in the future at a high price to make a profit is known as hedging.

5. The bulk of spot market transactions take place in the wholesale market known as the interbank market.

6. The effective exchange rate (EER) embodies the changes in prices in the two countries in he calculation.

7. Absolute purchasing power parity is a weaker version of PPP that relates the change in the exchange rate to changes in price levels in the two countries.

8. If a speculator expects the actual future spot rate will be higher than the current forward rate, the speculator will take a long position in foreign exchange.

9. When the exchange rate is expressed in terms of domestic currency units per unit of foreign currency, the foreign currency is at discount whenever the forward rate is higher than the spot rate.

10. Capital market imperfections, differential costs in gathering information about alternative investments, and the noncomparability of assets all can contribute to the existence of interest rate differentials between countries beyond the explained by covered interest arbitrage.

FILL-IN QUESTIONS

1. The price of one currency in terms of another is known as the _____.

2. The _____ is a worldwide network of markets and institutions that handle the exchange of foreign currencies.

3. A decrease in the home currency price of the foreign currency is known as home currency _____ or foreign currency _____.

4. An increase in the home currency price of the foreign currency is known as home currency _____ or foreign currency _____.

5. A multicurrency arbitrage that involves an inconsistency between three different currencies is known as _____.

6. The purchasing power parity approach rests on the postulate that any given commodity tends to have the same price worldwide when measured in the same currency or the law of _____.

7. The difference between the buying and selling price of foreign currency is known as the _____.

8. If a speculator expects that the actual future spot rate will be less than the current forward rate, the speculator will take a _____ position in foreign exchange.

9. The three elements considered by an investor when deciding whether to invest at home or abroad are:
   1. _____
   2. _____
   3. _____

10. _____ achieves equality conditions between domestic and foreign investment by linking the spot market, forward markets, and money markets.

DISCUSSION QUESTIONS

1. Explain the difference between the spot market, the forward market, and the futures market in foreign exchange.

2. Discuss the principal reasons people demand foreign currency.

3. Discuss the principal reasons foreign currency is supplied to the home country.

4. Discuss the role of arbitrage in promoting consistency in exchange rates across different markets.

5. Compare and contrast the use of the forward markets and futures market for hedging and speculation.

6. Compare and contrast the effective exchange rate, real exchange rate, and real effective exchange rate as measures of the strength of a country's currency.

7. Discuss purchasing power parity (PPP) and the law of one price. Why is relative purchasing power parity considered a weaker version of PPP?

8. Discuss the equilibrium condition in international financial markets known as uncovered interest parity. How does the addition of a risk premium change this condition? How does the investor move to a covered interest parity position?

9. Discuss the international financial and exchange rate adjustments by examining the spot market, forward market, domestic money market, and foreign money market.

PROBLEMS

1. Given the following information:

Country	eI^i	W_i
Mexico	1.27	.20
Canada	.91	.36
Japan	1.13	.24
Germany	.87	.11
U.K.	.78	.09

compute the effective exchange rate (EER).

2. Calculate the real exchange rate (RER) for 1994 given:
$e_{1994} = \$.025/p$

$PI^{Mex}_{1994} = 118.5$

$PI^{US}_{1994} = 105.$

3. Given the following information:

Country	RER-Index	W_i
Mexico	.94	.24
Canada	.89	.48
Japan	1.31	.28

Calculate the real effective exchange rate (REER).

4. Using the U.S. and Japan examine the parity condition for a 90 day investment of $1.
   If e = $.5/yen
   annual i_{NY} = 10%
   annual i_{Tokyo} = 16%

find the E(e) that will maintain the parity condition.

CASE STUDY QUESTIONS
Refer to Case Study 1 (p. 435) The Big Mac Index

1. How does the Big Mac Index differ from other PPP measures of the "true equivalent value" of a particular economy? What impact would you expect this to have on the BMI's accuracy?

2. Using the BMI calculations from the table, what conclusions can be reached about the European currencies?

3. Discuss the assumptions that must be made to construct the BMI. What adjustments would have been necessary if the U.S. price reduction of 65 percent had become permanent?

Refer to Case Study 2 (p. 436) Spot and PPP Exchange Rates Mark/Dollar and Yen/Dollar, 1973-1996

1. Discuss the difference between the spot exchange rate and the relative PPP rate.

2. What is happening to relative prices in the US and Germany to explain the divergences between the spot rates and PPP rates between 1981 and 1987?

3. What is happening to relative prices in the U.S. and Japan to explain the divergences between the spot rates and PPP rates between 1978 and 1986?

4. In both cases what has been the long-term trend of the U.S. dollar relative to the deutsche mark and the yen?

ANSWERS

True/False Questions
1. False
2. False
3. True
4. False
5. True
6. False
7. False
8. True
9. False
10. True

Fill-in questions
1. foreign exchange rate
2. foreign exchange market
3. appreciation; depreciation
4. depreciation; appreciation
5. triangular arbitrage
6. one price
7. retail spread or retail trading margin
8. short
9. 1. the domestic interest rate
   2. the foreign interest rate
   3. any expected changes in the exchange rate
10. covered interest arbitrage

Problems

1. $EER = (1.27)(.20) + (.91)(.36) + (1.13)(.24) + (.87)(.11) + (.78)(.09)$
   $= (.254) + (.328) + (.271) + (.096) + (.07)$
   $= 1.019$

2. $RER_{\$/p} = (.025/p)(118.5/105) =$
   $= (.025/p)(1.129) =$
   $= 0.028$

3. $REER = (.94)(.24) + (.89)(.48) + (1.31)(.28)$
   $= (.226) + (.427) + (.367)$
   $= 1.02$

4. annual interest rate in NY = 10%; 90 day rate = 2.5%
   annual interest rate in Tokyo = 16%; 90 day rate = 4%
   $(1 + i_{ny})/(1 + i_{Tokyo}) = E(e)/e$
   $(1 + .025)/(1 + .04) = E(e)/.5$
   $(.986)(.5) = E(e)$
   An expected 90 day spot rate of .493 would make the two investments equivalent.

CHAPTER 22
International Financial Markets and Instruments: An Introduction

SUMMARY

Over the last several decades, depositors have increasingly been seeking international outlets for their savings and banks increasingly seek international borrowers for their funds. This cross-border bank activity is not necessarily denominated in the home currency of the bank. The U.S. dollar is by far the leading currency of denomination of foreign assets, but the deutsche mark and the yen have been growing in importance (see Table 2).

International bank lending (loans across country borders) occurs in a variety of forms. The three most prevalent are loans made to non-residents in domestic currency, loans made to non-residents in foreign currency, and loans made to domestic residents in foreign currency. This use of currency outside the country in which it was issued has been dubbed as activity in the Eurocurrency market.

The Eurocurrency market really began to gain significance during the 1950's. The Cold War led the Soviet Union to find banks outside the U.S. to hold their foreign deposits. Changes in U.S. banking and tax regulations in the 1960's continued to push dollar-based deposits outside the U.S. These foreign currency denominated accounts in the so-called Eurobanks became the basis of greater expansion in the Eurocurrency market. The Eurobank funds were available for loans and subject to a deposit expansion multiplier effect. In the 1970's, OPEC oil deposits in Eurobanks led to significant increases in the supply of Eurocurrency.

This growth was not limited to currency, but also occurred in the bond market. U.S. restrictions on income from foreign bonds and lending restraints pushed bond issuers to Europe. The relaxation of capital controls in Europe allowed the market to expand. When the bonds are issued in one foreign country the activity is said to be in the foreign bond market. The issuing of bonds in multiple foreign countries is referred to as the Eurobond market. With the globalization of major economies, there is no reason to expect retrenchment in the Eurocurrency or Eurobond markets. In fact, continued growth is expected in both. The existence of the Eurocurrency and Eurobond markets have significant impacts on financial markets. The increased mobility of financial capital puts pressure on interest rates to equalize across countries. The greater mobility also leads to a more efficient allocation of financial capital. The existence of these two markets also increases the level of activity in the foreign currency markets. Finally, there is a concern that internationalization of these financial markets may reduce the independence of a nation's monetary authority. In recent years, this increased mobility of financial capital, the spread of MNCs, and the growth of stock exchanges in developing countries have led to international stock purchases and the development of international mutual funds.

When comparing the expected returns on domestic financial assets to foreign assets, two sources of risk must be considered. The first is the risk associated with the exchange rate and the second is the interest rate risk if there is a period of time before the transaction is completed. A comparison of rates between U.S. banks and Eurobanks shows that deposit rates are consistently higher in the Eurobanks and Eurobank lending rates are consistently lower. These differences are related to the foreign risk differential, but are also tied to differences in institutional costs.

Financial institutions have also developed a variety of new instruments to spread risk related to exchange rates and future interest rates.
These instruments include:

1. maturity mismatching
2. future rate agreements
3. Eurodollar interest rate swaps
4. Eurodollar cross-currency interest rate swap
5. Eurodollar interest rate futures
6. Eurodollar interest rate options
7. Options on swaps
8. equity financial derivatives

The growth in the Eurocurrency derivatives market has been related to the ability of international investors to increase their returns and lower their risk exposure. Administrative changes have also increased the ability of lenders to control their risks. The creation of loan syndicates protect the banks from excessive exposure to credit risk and allows access to large amounts of funds more rapidly and often at a lower cost.

DEFINE THE FOLLOWING KEY TERMS
basis points (p. 479)

bond underwriters (p. 462)

derivatives (p. 477)

direct loan syndicate (p. 489)

emerging market funds (p. 471)

Eurobanks (p. 458)

Eurobond markets (p. 462)

Eurocurrency market (p. 458)

Eurodollar call option (p. 483)

Eurodollar cross-currency interest rate swap (p. 480)

Eurodollar interest rate futures (p. 481)

Eurodollar interest rate option (p. 483)

Eurodollar interest rate swap (p. 480)

Eurodollar market (p. 458)

Eurodollar put option (p. 483)

Eurodollar strip (p. 483)

Euronotes (p. 463)

foreign bond markets (p. 462)

future rate agreement (p. 479)

global funds (p. 471)

gross international bank lending (p. 456)

international bank lending (p. 456)

international bond market (p. 461)

international funds (p. 471)

international portfolio diversification (p. 469)

loan participation syndicate (p. 489)

London Interbank Offered Rate (LIBOR) (p. 459)

maturity mismatching (p. 479)

mutual funds (p. 471)

net international bank lending (p. 457)

options on swaps (p. 486)

regional funds (p. 471)

traditional foreign bank lending (p. 457)

TRUE/FALSE QUESTIONS

1. The continued economic integration in Europe has resulted in the European Currency Unit (ECU) replacing the U.S. dollar as the leading currency of denomination of foreign assets.

2. The London Interbank Offered Rate (LIBOR) is the rate at which Eurobanks lend among themselves.

3. When a borrower in one country issues bonds in the markets of many countries with the help of a multinational loan syndicate, the activity is in the Eurobond market.

4. Eurobonds with a maturity of greater than 10 years at issuance are called Euronotes.

5. An international mutual fund that focuses on securities of companies in particular geographic areas or countries would be known as a closed area fund.

6. The presence of the Eurocurrency market assures that interest rates are equalized for all nations involved in international trade.

7. The fact that banks are not subject to reserve requirements or deposit insurance assessments on Eurocurrency deposits helps explain why deposit rates on Eurocurrency accounts exceed domestic deposit rates.

8. A future rate agreement is essentially a contract between two parties to lock in a given interest rate starting at some given point in the future for some given time.

9. The buyer of a Eurodollar put option obtains the right to purchase a Eurodollar time deposit bearing a certain interest rate on a specific date.

10. In the case of a direct loan syndicate, participating banks sign a common loan agreement and essentially become co-lenders.

FILL-IN QUESTIONS

1. Domestic bank loans in domestic currency to nonresidents are generally referred to as _____ bank lending.

2. When a borrower in one country issues bonds in the market of one other country the transaction is said to be taking place in the _____.

3. A force that may generate a common trend movement of stock price indexes across countries is the phenomenon of _____ to reduce risk in investor's portfolios

4. _____ funds purchase packages of equities that contain stocks of corporations both in the U.S. and in other countries.

5. Maturity _____ is one of the easiest ways for financial institutions to remove the risk of changes in the interest rate between now and some future time.

6. The _____ is a financial derivative that permits the holder of a floating interest rate investment in one currency to change it into a fixed rate investment in another.

7. Contracts to deliver a certain amount of foreign currency denominated bank deposits at some future date that are traded on the Chicago Mercantile Exchange are known as _____.

8. The investor who purchases a Eurodollar ____ option acquires the right to sell a Eurodollar time deposit to the option writer at a specified interest rate at a future date.

9. A collection of multiple short term three-month futures contracts to hedge changes in interest rates for a longer period is referred to as a _____.

10. In a _____ syndicate, a lead bank usually executes the loan instrument with the

borrower and then syndicates the loan by entering into participation agreements with other banks.

DISCUSSION QUESTIONS

1. Discuss the three components of gross international bank lending and the reasons for the growth of this aspect of banking.

2. Using the case of a U.S. exporter selling goods to a British buyer and depositing the dollar payment in a British bank, track the eurodollar flow through the banking system and include a discussion of the bank deposit expansion.

3. Discuss the impact of a reduction in the discount rate by the Federal Reserve on domestic banks and Eurobanks.

4. Discuss the process of international portfolio diversification as a means to reduce risk in an investor's portfolio. Distinguish between global, international, emerging market, and regional mutual funds as potential additions to a diversifies portfolio.

5. In a comparison of returns on foreign investments, discuss the roles of exchange rates, interest rate risk, and transaction costs.

6. The integration of international financial markets has led to the development of a variety of new financial instruments that can be used to hedge against unforeseen interest rate changes. Discuss available options to remove the risk of interest rate changes between the time of the initial transaction and the completion of the deal in one year.

7. Discuss the use of the futures market in order to lock into a specific future interest rate in Eurocurrencies.

8. Discuss the use of loan syndicates as a means to involve smaller and less well informed banks in the international lending process.

9. Explain the role of the Eurocurrency, Eurobond, and international stock markets in improving the efficiency with which capital is allocated.

CASE STUDY QUESTIONS
Refer to Case Study 1 (p. 465) Interest Rates Across Countries

1. Discuss the need to use the real yield as opposed to nominal yield in making interest rate comparisons between nations.

2. Using the differences between real yields in developed and developing countries, discuss the importance of being integrated into the world financial system.

3. Do the nations with negative real returns share any common characteristics? Explain the role of these characteristics in their bond market.

Refer to Case Study 2 (p. 468) Stock Market Performance in Developing Countries

1. List the factors responsible for the surge in stock purchases in the developing countries.

2. What region of the world seems to have experienced the most dramatic growth their stock price indexes during this period? What factor have contributed to this growth?

3. What is the impact of political or economic unrest in a nation on stock market performance? Discuss two examples.

Refer to Case Study 3 (p. 475) U.S. Domestic and Eurodollar Deposit and Lending Rates, 1989-1996

1. Using the diagrams of deposit and lending rates in U.S. banks and Eurobanks, discuss the degree of financial integration between these markets.

2. Discuss the role of risk in determining the differences between deposit rates in these two sets of institutions.

3. Discuss the roles of required reserve ratios and deposit insurance in determining the differences between lending rates in the two institutions.

ANSWERS

True/False Questions

1. False
2. True
3. True
4. False
5. False
6. False
7. True
8. True
9. False
10. True

Fill-in questions

1. traditional foreign
2. foreign bond market
3. international portfolio diversification
4. Global
5. mismatching
6. Eurodollar cross-currency interest rate swap
7. Eurodollar interest rate futures
8. put
9. Eurodollar strips
10. loan participation

CHAPTER 23
The Monetary and Portfolio Balance Approaches to External Balance

SUMMARY

This chapter examines two broad, aggregate approaches to the determination of a country's balance of payments position and exchange rate. The first approach is known as the monetary approach to the balance of payments. This approach analyzes a country's balance of payments in terms of a country's supply of and demand for money. The money supply usually deals with either M1 or M2 and the most important assets are domestic reserves and international reserves. Money demand is a function of income, price level, the interest rate, the level of wealth, expected change in prices, as well as other variables. The simple equation for monetary equilibrium is

$$M_S = kPY.$$

Changes in the money market have a variety of impacts on the balance of payments (BOP). With fixed exchange rates, an excess supply of money leads people to reduce their cash balances. In terms of the BOP, the excess cash balances lead to a current account deficit and a deficit in the private capital account. These actions all increase the demand for money and ultimately bring the BOP back in line. This monetary approach works in reverse in the case of an excess demand for money.

The monetary approach is also used in exchange rate determination. By moving from a fixed exchange rate to a model with flexible exchange rates, BOP surpluses and deficits are eliminated by changes in the exchange rate. The flexible rate case parallels the fixed exchange rate case except that "BOP deficit" is replaced by depreciation of the home currency and "BOP surplus" is replaced by appreciation of the home currency. In a two country case, changes in the growth of the money supply in either country can impact the exchange rate so that the nation printing money the fastest will see its currency depreciate. The empirical tests of the monetary approach have led to sharply contrasting conclusions.

The second major approach is the portfolio balance or asset market approach. These models share the following characteristics:

(1) financial markets are extremely well integrated
(2) domestic and foreign assets are imperfect substitutes
(3) asset holders attempt to maximize their return by switching assets to achieve higher expected returns.
(4) investors have rational expectations.

The models examine the supply and demand for money, domestic bonds, and foreign bonds. In the case of a contraction of the home money supply, the results include increases in the home country interest rate, the foreign interest rate and the expected depreciation of the home currency. In the case of inflationary expectations, the outcome includes a depreciation of the home currency and an increase in the demand for foreign bonds. Continuing in the portfolio balance models, an increase in real income in the home country results in increased demand for money, sales of domestic and foreign bonds, and an appreciation of the home country currency. An increase in home country wealth can occur in two ways. If the wealth increase is from an increase in the domestic bond supply, domestic bond prices will fall and the domestic interest rate will rise. While the increase in wealth may lead to an increase in the demand for foreign bonds, the capital inflow due to the higher interest rates is expected to be relatively stronger leading to a net appreciation in the home currency. If the wealth increase is from a home country current account surplus, the net impact on home currency is indeterminant. Finally, an increase in the supply of foreign bonds leads to an appreciation of the home currency, a fall in the price of foreign bonds and an increase in the risk premium. The BOP surplus or deficit or the appreciation or depreciation of the home currency are only temporary. Once the desired portfolios have been achieved and asset stock equilibrium is reached all imbalances cease.

The Dornbusch model examines the relationship between the exchange rate and the price level in the long run. This model is used to address exchange rate overshooting. In response to an increase in the money supply, the Dornbusch model predicts excess depreciation of the home currency due to price rigidity. As prices begin to adjust, the exchange rate appreciates to the long run equilibrium level. The same type of overshooting can take place when the forward market for foreign exchange is added to the examination. These results emphasize that the complexity of the real world means that exchange rates do not move smoothly from one equilibrium to another.

DEFINE THE FOLLOWING KEY TERMS
asset stock equilibrium (p. 511)

demand for money (p. 493)

domestic credit issued by the central bank or domestic reserves (p. 492)

efficient exchange market (p. 517)

exchange rate overshooting (p. 513)

incipient BOP deficit (p. 498)

incipient BOP surplus (p. 499)

international reserves (p. 492)

monetary approach to the balance of payments (p. 491)

monetary approach to the exchange rate (p. 498)

monetary base (p. 492)

money multiplier (p. 492)

portfolio balance or asset market approach (p. 505)

rational expectations (p. 505)

transactions demand for money (p. 494)

TRUE/FALSE QUESTIONS
1. The belief that a country's balance of payments is essentially a monetary phenomena is known as the asset market approach.

2. While the money supply has various definitions, the monetary approach usually deals with either M1 or M2.

3. The sum of reserves held by banks plus currency outside banks is usually called the monetary base.

4. In the monetary approach to the balance of payments, an excess supply of money generates pressures leading to a current account surplus.

5. In the monetary approach to the balance of payments, under fixed exchange rates disequilibria in the money market and BOP deficits or surpluses will exist in the long run.

6. The results of the separate analyses by Frenkel and Dornbusch prove that the monetary approach to exchange rate determination is clearly valid after 1978.

7. Rational expectations assumes forward-looking, utility-maximizing investors utilize all available relevant information and knowledge of how the economy and exchange markets work in order to form forecasts.

8. Under a flexible exchange rate assumption in the portfolio balance approach, an increase in real income in the home country leads to an appreciation of the home currency.

9. Under a flexible exchange rate assumption in the portfolio balance approach, an increase in the supply of foreign bonds would serve to appreciate the foreign currency.

10. Exchange rate overshooting occurs when, in moving from one equilibrium to another, the exchange rate goes beyond the new equilibrium but then returns to it.

FILL-IN QUESTIONS

1. The amount of bank deposits is a function of the amount of reserves of commercial banks and the _____.

2. As income rises, individuals want to spend more on consumption. The money needed to finance this additional consumption is known as the _____ demand for money.

3. With a flexible exchange rate, an increase in the money supply leads to an _____ and therefore a fall in the value of the home currency.

4. If a country is "printing money" faster than its trading partners, its currency will _____; if a country is more restrictive with respect to its monetary growth than its trading partners, its currency will _____.

5. An extension of the monetary approach to BOP and exchange rate determination to include other financial assets besides money is known as the _____ approach.

6. MacDonald and Taylor (1992) define the wealth of the domestic country in terms of its own currency as the _____ of the home country plus the stock of _____ held by domestic residents plus the stock of _____ held by domestic residents.

7. A BOP deficit or surplus will not exist once _____ has been achieved.

8. In the Dornbusch model, goods prices are assumed to be _____ in the short run meaning they adjust slowly to changing conditions.

9. In the Dornbusch model, an increase in the home money supply can result in _____ the exchange rate when the forward market for foreign exchange is considered.

10. When the expected future spot rate [E(e)] is equal to the current forward rate (e_{fwd}), the exchange market is said to be an _____.

DISCUSSION QUESTIONS

1. Suppose the central bank purchases government securities through open market operations. Explain the impact on the money supply. Would the results change if the central bank purchased foreign exchange from an exporter? Why or why not?

2. Discuss the predicted relationships between Y, P, i, W, E(p) and L (the demand for money).

3. Using the monetary approach to BOP with a fixed exchange rate, discuss the impact of a decrease in the money supply on the nations:
   a) current account
   b) private capital account
   c) BOP surplus or deficit
   d) expected inflation rate

4. Using the monetary approach to the exchange rate describe the cause and result of an incipient BOP surplus.

5. List and explain the overriding characteristics of a portfolio balance approach to BOP and exchange rate determination.

6. Discuss the differences between the money demand functions in the monetary and portfolio balance approaches to BOP determination.

7. In the portfolio balance approach to BOP determination, discuss the impact of an expansion of the home money supply and a decrease in the domestic bond supply.

8. Discuss exchange rate overshooting in the context of an increase in the money supply in the Dornbusch model.

PROBLEMS
1. Given the following information:
   BR = 560
   C = 340
   a = 4

   a) Determine the nation's money supply.

   b) Determine the nation's monetary base.

2. Using the monetary approach in a two country framework, assume the price level in country A is $100 and the price level in country B is 200p. Given $P_A = eP_B$, find the exchange rate (e).

3. Given: the money supply in the home country is $3000
   the stock of home bonds held by domestic residents is $1000
   the stock of foreign bonds held by domestic residents is 20,000p
   the exchange rate is $.10/p.

Find the domestic wealth in terms of its own currency.

CASE STUDY QUESTIONS
Refer to Case Study 1 (p. 493) Relationships Between Monetary Concepts in the United States

1. In Table 1, why are Federal Reserve notes and deposits of financial institutions considered to be liabilities?

2. Why would assets in foreign currencies be considered assets for the U.S. Federal Reserve?

3. What would happen to the money supply if the average reserves of all depository institutions increased by $1 billion?

ANSWERS

True/False Questions
1. False
2. True
3. True
4. False
5. False
6. False
7. True
8. True
9. False
10. True

Fill-in questions
1. money multiplier
2. transaction
3. incipient BOP deficit
4. depreciate; appreciate
5. portfolio balance or asset market
6. money supply; home bonds; foreign bonds
7. asset stock equilibrium
8. sticky
9. overshooting
10. efficient exchange market

Problems
1. a. $M_S = a(BR + C)$
       $= 4(560 + 340)$
       $= 4(900)$
       $= \$3600$

   b. monetary base $= BR + C$
       $= 560 + 340$
       $= \$900$

2. $e = P_A/P_B$
   $= \$100/200p$
   $= \$.5/p$

3. $W_d = M_S + B_h + eB_o$
   $= \$3000 + \$1000 + (.10)(20,000)$
   $= \$3000 + \$1000 + \$2000$
   $= \$6000$

CHAPTER 24
Price Adjustments to Balance of Payments Disequilibrium

SUMMARY

This chapter focuses on the foreign exchange market. In the simplified case of the price adjustment mechanism, a current account deficit would lead to a depreciation of the home currency. The depreciation causes foreign prices to increase reducing imports and it also reduces the price of home goods to foreigners increasing exports (expenditure switching).

In terms of the supply and demand for foreign exchange, it is important to note that the demand for foreign exchange is a derived demand. Demand for foreign goods and services is responsive to changes in the exchange rate because $P_{Home} = P_{Foreign} \times e$. The analysis of the foreign exchange market focuses on stability and the impact of a change in the exchange rate on the nation's current account balance.

Stability in the foreign exchange market requires that market forces will react to nonequilibrium exchange rates and move them back to equilibrium. If foreign demand for home goods (resulting in the supply of foreign currency) is elastic, the normal upward sloping supply curve will result in market stability. If the foreign demand for home goods in inelastic, the result is a backward bending supply of foreign exchange and questions about stability.

Market stability and the impact of exchange rate changes on the current account are a function of the elasticity of demand for foreign exchange relative to the elasticity of supply. If the home country's demand for foreign exchange is elastic, the current account unambiguously improves with depreciation. The cases of inelastic home country demand for foreign exchange are more ambiguous. As long as the increase in foreign expenditures more than offset increased domestic expenditures on imports, the current account balance improves with depreciation and the foreign exchange market is stable. This occurs when the sum of foreign and domestic elasticities of demand for imports is greater than one - known as meeting the Marshal-Lerner condition. Violation of this condition results in instability in the foreign exchange market.

While this price adjustment mechanism seems to function with certain regularity in long run situations, the short run effects are relatively more volatile and less certain. In terms of the exchange rate, a current account deficit is expected to result in a depreciation of the currency. In many cases, consumers and producers are unresponsive to the changes in the short run. The lack of adjustment to the depreciation actually makes the deficit worse in the short run. Given more time the expected adjustment takes place and the deficit is eliminated. The lagged response causes the current account balance to go down before going up and the impact is referred to as the J curve.

The alternative to a flexible exchange rate is a system of fixed exchange rates. These systems require a substantial supply of international assets and flexible prices. One popular version is the gold standard. All exchange rates are fixed and linked by fixing the value of their currency relative to gold. Another fixed exchange rate system uses pegged exchange rates. Under this system the value of the domestic currency is fixed relative to an international currency or basket of currencies. The monetary authorities must stand ready to buy or sell international reserve assets in response to changes in the supply or demand for their currency.

DEFINE THE FOLLOWING KEY TERMS

complete exchange rate pass-through (p. 536)

elasticities approach (p. 524)

elasticity of exchange rate pass-through (p. 537)

expenditure switching (p. 524)

gold export point (p. 542)

gold import point (p. 542)

gold standard (p. 541)

J curve (p. 539)

market stability (p. 527)

Marshall-Lerner condition (p. 533)

mint par (p. 541)

partial exchange rate pass-through (p. 537)

pegged rate system (p. 543)

price adjustment mechanism (p. 524)

"rules of the game" (p. 541)

TRUE/FALSE QUESTIONS

1. The demand for foreign exchange is a derived demand.

2. Since the demand for foreign currency by the home country is simply the supply of home currency to the foreign country, if one knows the demand for foreign currency in each of the two countries, the supply of foreign exchange to each is also known.

3. In the foreign exchange market with a backward-sloping supply curve, if the supply curve is steeper than the demand curve the market is unstable with respect to price.

4. If foreign demand for home goods is elastic, the supply curve of foreign exchange is backward-sloping.

5. If the increased domestic expenditures on imports is greater than the increase in expenditures on home country exports, the current account balance will worsen with depreciation and the foreign exchange market will be unstable.

6. The Marshall-Lerner condition requires that the sum of the foreign and domestic elasticities of demand for imports be greater than one.

7. The J curve suggests that if consumers and producers are unresponsive in the short run, a depreciation actually leads to a short run worsening in the current account before it ultimately gets better.

8. The income elasticity of demand for imports is the percentage change in income divided by the percentage change in the demand for imports.

9. If the elasticity of exchange rate pass-through is greater than 1, then there is partial exchange rate pass-through.

10. The upper break-even price under a gold standard at which the supply and demand for the foreign currency become perfectly elastic is referred to as the gold import point.

FILL-IN QUESTIONS

1. The adjustment to changes in relative prices brought about by changes in the exchange rate is called the _____ to adjustment in the foreign exchange market.

2. _____ is reflected in the tendency of foreign buyers to switch expenditures from their own products to cheaper imports when a trading partner depreciates its currency.

3. _____ occurs when the characteristics of supply and demand are such that any deviation away from equilibrium sets in motion forces that move the market back toward equilibrium.

4. The general condition for exchange market stability is referred to as the _____.

5. In the case of a _____, currencies are valued in gold, and all currencies that are pegged to gold are therefore linked to each other.

6. If the dollar is fixed at $100 per ounce of gold and the pound sterling is fixed at 25 pounds per ounce of gold, then the dollar/pound _____ exchange rate is $4/pound.

7. The upper break-even price at which the supply and demand for the currency become perfectly elastic is often referred to as the _____.

8. Under a _____, governments fix the price of their currency to an internationally accepted asset and stand ready to support the fixed price in the foreign exchange market.

9. _____ occurs when the exchange rate change is allowed to register its full impact on the foreign consumer price of the good..

10. The elasticity of _____ is the percentage change in the import price index for a good divided by the percentage change in the (nominal effective) exchange rate.

DISCUSSION QUESTIONS

1. Discuss the characteristics of the demand and supply for foreign exchange. Explain why the demand for foreign exchange is considered to be a derived demand.

2. Explain the existence of a backward sloping supply curve for foreign exchange. Discuss the relationship between price elasticity of demand for imports and market stability.

3. Discuss the conditions under which the depreciation of a currency would lead to a J curve.

4. Define a gold standard. Discuss the price adjustment mechanism within this system.

PROBLEMS

1. Given the following:

   $P_1 = \$10$
   $P_2 = \$12$
   $Q_1 = 200$
   $Q_2 = 100$;

   use the arc method to compute the price elasticity of demand.

2. Given the following information

Country	Import Price Elasticity	Export Price Elasticity
Canada	-1.04	-.81
Germany	-.72	-.69
Italy	-.41	-.43

   Use the Marshall-Lerner condition to determine the answers to each question.

   a. Is the foreign exchange market stable in Canada?
   b. Is the foreign exchange market stable in Germany?
   c. Is the foreign exchange market stable in Italy?

CASE STUDY QUESTIONS
Refer to Case Study #1 (p. 534) Estimates of Import and Export Demand Elasticities

1. Define the Marshall - Lerner condition. What does this condition mean for exchange rate market stability in the countries listed in Table 3.

2. What are the characteristics of the supply of foreign exchange in the U.K.? What is true of the relationship between the demand and supply of foreign exchange in the U.K.?

3. Would the conditions described in #2 be expected to continue for the U.K. in the long run?

4. Would the other nations in Table 3 be expected to move from stability to instability in the long run? Why or why not?

Refer to Case Study #2 (p. 536) U.S. and Foreign Exporters' Price/Cost Ratios, "Pass-Through," and the Exchange Rate

1. Why would economists expect that price/cost ratios would move in sympathy with exchange rates?

2. Given the information in the chart, what is happening to the prices paid by buyers?

3. What does this information mean about the response of U.S. imports to changes in the value of the dollar?

4. In the case of the U.S. is complete exchange rate pass-through occurring? According to Yang, should we expect the pass-through to be complete? Why or why not?

Refer to Case Study #3 (p. 540) Lagged Response of Net Exports to Exchange Rate Changes

1. Describe the expected changes in real net exports as the exchange rate depreciates? As it appreciates?

2. Discuss the concept of the J curve.

3. Does the information in the chart support the existence of a J curve? Why or why not?

ANSWERS

True/False Questions
1. True
2. True
3. False
4. False
5. True
6. True
7. True
8. False
9. False
10. False

Fill-in questions
1. elasticities approach
2. Expenditure switching
3. Market stability
4. Marshall-Lerner condition
5. gold standard
6. mint par
7. gold export point
8. pegged exchange rate system
9. Complete exchange rate pass-through
10. exchange rate pass-through

Problems
1. $((100 - 200 / (100 + 200)/2) / (12-10 / (12 + 10) /2))$
   $(-100 / 150) / (2/11)$
   $(-2/3) / (2/11)$
   $-11/3$ elastic demand

2. a. Canada is stable (M-L condition is satisfied)
   b. Germany is stable (M-L condition is satisfied)
   c. Italy is not stable (M-L condition is not satisfied)

CHAPTER 25
National Income and the Current Account

SUMMARY

To examine the relationship between national income and the external sector, an open economy Keynesian income model is utilized. The basis of the model is that desired expenditures or aggregate demand is equal to consumption plus investment plus government expenditures plus net exports (exports - imports). The open nature of the model brings the autonomous exports and imports into the equality. Imports are assumed to be a function of income (similar to consumption). Equilibrium occurs when desired spending (C + I + G + (X - M)) is equal to production. By the leakages and injection approach, equilibrium occurs when the leakages (saving + taxes + imports) are equal to the injections (investment + government spending + exports).

Autonomous changes in expenditures have a multiple effect on economic activity. The open economy multiplier is written as 1/1 - [MPC (1 - t) - MPM] where MPC is the marginal propensity to consume, t is the tax rate, and MPM is the marginal propensity to import. Changes in investment, government expenditures, and exports have a positive multiplier effect on the economy. An increase in autonomous imports would have a negative multiplier effect on the economy.

Policy decisions must account for the multiplier effect. Attempts to decrease imports by reducing income will have large impacts on internal targets (income and employment) as a result of meeting external (current account balance) targets. Efforts to increase exports must account for the fact that as exports increase income, consumers will increase imports. The open economy Keynesian income model complicates policy decisions. This is particularly true if the foreign repercussions of policy decisions are considered.

The examination of macroeconomic goals of internal and external balances can lead to cases where monetary and fiscal policy actions are not clear. For example, the existence of a current account deficit and high unemployment cannot be corrected by the same monetary or fiscal policy action. The same would be true of a current account surplus and rapid inflation. In these instances, the exchange rate is used as an instrument of policy. The Swan framework is used to illustrate the fact that simultaneously meeting the goals of external and internal balance requires the use of exchange rate changes and macroeconomic policy. The model points out that only one exchange rate permits the attainment of both targets. The major criticism of the model is that it is difficult to know the exact internal and external balance relationships and therefore difficult to find the equilibrium.

DEFINE THE FOLLOWING KEY TERMS

autonomous consumption spending (p. 549)

autonomous imports (p. 553)

autonomous spending multiplier (p. 560)

average propensity to import (APM) (p. 553)

consumption function (p. 549)

desired aggregate expenditures (p. 547)

equilibrium level of national income (p. 555)

external balance (p. 566)

foreign repercussions (p. 564)

import function (p. 553)

income elasticity of demand for imports (YEM) (p. 553)

induced consumption spending (p. 549)

induced imports (p. 553)

injections (p. 557)

internal balance (p. 566)

Keynesian income model (p. 547)

leakages (p. 557)

marginal propensity to consume (MPC) (p. 549)

marginal propensity to import (MPM) (p. 553)

marginal propensity to save (MPS) (p. 549)

open-economy multiplier (p. 561)

open-economy multiplier with foreign repercussions (p. 564)

partial current account adjustment (p. 564)

rounds of spending in the multiplier process (p. 560)

saving function (p. 549)

TRUE/FALSE QUESTIONS

1. In the Keynesian income model, desired aggregate expenditures can be written as $E = C + I + G + X + M$.

2. The part of the consumption function that depends on current income is known as induced consumption spending.

3. In the simple income model, investment is usually assumed to be autonomous or independent of current national income.

4. The marginal propensity to import is defined as the change in imports divided by the change in exports.

5. The income elasticity of demand for imports is the percentage change in income divided by the percentage change in imports.

6. In the leakages and injections model, the economy is in equilibrium when $S + T + X = I + G + M$.

7. The autonomous spending multiplier is used to explain the process by which changes in C, I, G, or X result in larger changes in equilibrium income.

8. With fixed exchange rates, policymakers when faced with a current account deficit and rapid inflation will use contractionary aggregate demand-oriented monetary and fiscal policy.

9. In the Swan model, the external balance goal is described by the downward sloping EB curve.

10. In the Swan model, only one exchange rate permits the simultaneous attainment of both external and internal balances.

FILL-IN QUESTIONS
Given the consumption function **C = 200 + 0.75 Y_d**, answer questions 1 & 2.

1. The marginal propensity to consume is equal to _____ in the above equation.

2. In the above equation, $ 200 is designated as the _____ consumption.

3. The relationship between imports and national income is expressed by the _____.

4. The level of income at which there is no tendency for the income level to rise or to fall is known as the _____ level of national income.

5. In determining the equilibrium level of national income, investment, government expenditures, and exports are considered _____ while saving, taxes and imports are considered _____.

6. An adjustment to an export increase that is less than the initial disturbance is called a _____ adjustment.

7. The balance in the current account (X = M) is known as _____ balance.

8. _____ balance refers to the desirable state of the economy where there is a low level of unemployment together with reasonable price stability.

9. In the Keynesian income models, spending and income changes that are transmitted to other countries through changes in imports of the home country are known as _____.

10. The Swan model assumes a _____ exchange rate system.

DISCUSSION QUESTIONS
1. Discuss the role of imports and exports in the Keynesian income model.

2. Explain the relationship between growth in imports and a country's national income growth using the income elasticity of demand for imports.

3. Explain the rounds of spending in the multiplier process. How is the process altered when the change is an increase in autonomous exports.

4. Discuss foreign repercussions in the Keynesian income model. What impact do these repercussions have on the multiplier?

5. Discuss the use of the Swan model to simultaneously address the possible conflict between the macroeconomic goals of external and internal balances.

PROBLEMS

1. Given the following consumption function: $C = 300 + 0.50\, Y_d$

   a. find autonomous consumption

   b. find the MPC

   c. find consumption when $Y_d = \$1000$

   d. find the MPS

   e. find autonomous saving

   f. determine the saving function

2. Given the following: $C = 200 + 0.8\, Y_d$
   $T = 0.25\, Y$
   $I = 200$
   $G = 600$
   $X = 170$
   $M = 20 + 0.10\, Y$

   a. when $Y = \$1000$, find taxes

   b. when $Y = \$1000$, find imports

   c. when $Y = \$1000$, find consumption

   d. find the equilibrium level of income

3. Given the following import function:

   M = 100 + 0.15Y

   a. Find the level of imports if Y = 2000.
   b. Find the level of imports if Y = 5000.
   c. Find the marginal propensity to import.

4. Given X = 200, M = 240, and MPM = .10 find the following

   a. the current account deficit
   b. the change in income necessary to balance the current account by decreasing imports.

CASE STUDY QUESTIONS
Refer to Case Study #1 (p. 554) Average Propensities to Import, Selected Countries

1. Given the APM data from Table 1, which nations appear to be more dependent on foreign trade.

2. What do the YEMs computed from the data suggest about each nation's elasticity of demand for imports?

3. Which markets appear to be the most promising for developing nations that are using an export oriented development program?

4. If each nation had a current account deficit of $100, use the crude MPMs to determine the change in income necessary to close the deficit by decreasing imports in each case.

Refer to Case Study #2 (p. 566) Income Interdependence Among Countries

1. Discuss the way foreign repercussions can lead to multiple changes in a variety of nations within the Keynesian income model.

2. Given the information in Table 2, explain which nations are most impacted by a shock in each of the following:
    a. the U.S.;

    b. Japan;

    c. Germany;

    d. Canada.

3. Given the information in Table 2, assess the impact if a recession in the U.S. on the other nations discussed in this case.

ANSWERS

True/False Questions
1. False
2. True
3. True
4. False
5. False
6. False
7. True
8. True
9. False
10. True

Fill-in questions
1. 0.75
2. autonomous
3. import function
4. equilibrium
5. injections ; leakages
6. partial current account
7. external
8. internal
9. foreign repercussions
10. pegged

Problems
1. a. $300
   b. 0.5
   c. $300 + 0.5 (1000) = 300 + 500 = 800$
   d. 0.5
   e. $-300
   f. $S = -300 + 0.5 Y_d$

2. a. $T = 0.25 (1000) = \$250$
   b. $M = 20 + .10 (1000) = 20 + 100 = \$120$
   c. $C = 200 + 0.8 (Y - .25 Y) = 200 + .8 (.75 (1000)) = 200 + 600 = \$800$
   d. $Y = C + I + G + X - M$
      $Y = 200 + .8 (Y - T) + 200 + 600 + 170 - 20 - .10 Y$
      $Y = 1150 + .8 (Y - .25Y) - .10Y$
      $Y = 1150 + .5 Y$
      $Y - .5 Y = 1150$
      $Y = \$2300$

3. a. $M = 100 + .15(2000) = 100 + 300 = 400$
   b. $M = 100 + .15(5000) = 100 + 750 = 850$
   c. .15

4. a. $X - M = 200 - 240 = -\$40$ (current account deficit of $40)
   b. $-40 = .10 \times$ change in income
   change in income = -400

CHAPTER 26
Economic Policy in the Open Economy: Fixed Exchange Rates

SUMMARY

This chapter examines economic policy in the open economy when exchange rates are fixed. The basic framework used to begin the analysis will focus on the interaction of policies aimed at obtaining external balance and those aimed at domestic targets such as full employment and price stability. The examination uses a Mundell-Fleming diagram with interest rates (representing monetary policy) on the vertical axis and G-I (representing fiscal policy) on the horizontal axis. The inverse relationship between the two policy instruments is shown by the upward sloping internal balance (IB) and external balance (EB) curves. The model demonstrates that only one combination of policies achieves both internal and external balance. In search of the appropriate combination, monetary policy must be focused on the EB target with fiscal policy focused on the IB target.

To move toward the broader general equilibrium in the open economy, the IS/LM/BP model is used. The LM curve slopes upward and shows the various combinations of income and interest rate that produce equilibrium in the money market. The IS curve slopes downward and shows the various combinations of income and interest rate that produce equilibrium in the real sector of the economy. The intersection of the IS and LM curves provides the only combination of income and interest rate that simultaneously give equilibrium in both sectors of the economy.

The third relationship represented in this model are the combinations of interest rate and income that produce equilibrium in the balance of payments. The BP curve is upward sloping representing the need for higher interest rates to induce a capital inflow to offset increases in imports that result from increases in income. An upward sloping BP curve refers to the case of imperfect capital mobility. The two exceptions are the case of perfect capital mobility (a horizontal BP curve) and the case of perfect capital immobility (a vertical BP curve). The slope of the BP curve reflects the nature of capital mobility in the country.

The general equilibrium in the money market, the real sector, and the balance of payments occurs when all three curves intersect. Under the fixed exchange rate, a shock to the system that creates a surplus or deficit in the balance of payments will result in an automatic monetary adjustment that returns the economy to a state of equilibrium. As long as the exchange rate remains fixed, changes in the BOP will lead to adjustments in the domestic money supply.

An analysis of the effectiveness of fiscal policy begins with the economy in general equilibrium. The effectiveness of fiscal policy is determined by the degree of international capital mobility. In the case of perfect capital immobility (a vertical BP), the impact of expansionary fiscal policy is totally offset by the crowding out of domestic investment. As capital mobility increases, the extent of the crowding out is reduced to the point that expansionary fiscal policy has a small positive impact on income and employment. At the opposite extreme, the case of perfect capital mobility (a horizontal BP) expansionary fiscal policy is totally effective due to the complete absence of crowding out. The greater the mobility of capital, with fixed exchange rates, the greater the effectiveness of fiscal policy.

The effectiveness of expansionary monetary policy with fixed exchange rates must also be addressed. An increase in the money supply, represented by a rightward shift in the LM curve, results in a balance of payments deficit. In the absence of exchange rate adjustments, the BOP deficit forces the central bank to sell foreign exchange. Selling foreign exchange results in a decrease in the domestic money supply that shifts the LM curve back to the left. As a result, monetary policy is totally ineffective under fixed exchange rates regardless of the degree of capital mobility.

While the exchange rate is not an active tool of discretionary policy, adjustments in the pegged value of the currency are possible. Changing macroeconomic condition may necessitate a devaluation or appreciation of the home currency and the impacts should be examined. Changes in the exchange rate impact imports and exports resulting in adjustments of both IS and BP. While a depreciation of the home currency has a positive impact on income under all possible assumptions of capital mobility, the degree of mobility is important to consider. As with fiscal policy, the effect will be the greatest with perfect capital mobility where there are no crowding out effects.

DEFINE THE FOLLOWING KEY TERMS
automatic monetary adjustment (p. 594)

BP curve (p. 587)

crowding out (p. 595)

equilibrium interest rate (p. 581)

imperfect capital mobility (p. 589)

IS curve (p. 585)

LM curve (p. 583)

Mundell-Fleming diagram (p. 578)

perfect capital immobility (p. 590)

perfect capital mobility (p. 589)

relative capital immobility (p. 596)

relative capital mobility (p. 596)

sterilization (p. 594)

TRUE/FALSE QUESTIONS
1. External balance or "BOP equilibrium" was defined by Mundell to mean a zero balance in the current account.

2. In the Mundell-Fleming diagram, the IB curve is steeper than the EB curve because the changes in the money supply (and the interest rate) are assumed to have a greater effect on the external balance than on the internal balance.

3. Given the nature of the IB and EB functions, it is more efficient to assign the monetary policy instrument to pursue EB and fiscal policy instruments to pursue IB targets.

4. Any point to the right of the LM curve represents an excess supply of money.

5. Points on the IS curve represent combinations of income and the interest rate that make investment plus exports plus government spending equal to saving plus imports plus taxes.

6. Imperfect capital mobility between countries is represented by BP curves that are upward sloping.

7. A depreciation of the home currency against foreign currencies shifts the BP curve to the right.

8. Under a system of fixed exchange rates, expansionary fiscal policy is more effective under conditions of perfect capital immobility.

9. Under a system of fixed exchange rates, expansionary monetary policy is more effective under conditions of perfect capital mobility.

10. Devaluation of a pegged currency have an expansionary effect on the economy regardless of the capital mobility assumptions.

FILL-IN QUESTIONS
Consider the 4 quadrants of the Mundell-Fleming diagram in Figure 1 (p. 579) to answer questions 1 - 3.

1. A point in quadrant II of the diagram would be characterized by the existence of _____ and a _____.

2. The simultaneous existence of unemployment and a balance of payments deficit would characterize a point in quadrant _____.

3. Points above (or to the left) of the EB curve reflect a balance of payments _____.

4. The LM curve shows the various combinations of income and the interest rate that produce equilibrium in the _____.

5. The BP curve shows the various combinations of income and the interest rate that produce equilibrium in the _____.

6. The IS curve shows the various combinations of income and the interest rate that produce equilibrium in the _____ of the economy.

7. A vertical BP curve, indicating that barriers to capital movements are such that there is _____.

8. Central bank interference in the automatic monetary adjustment under a fixed exchange rate system is known as _____.

9. Increased government spending under conditions of perfectly immobile capital results in a _____ of an equivalent amount of domestic investment.

10. Monetary policy is completely _____ for influencing income in the IS/LM/BP model with fixed exchange rates.

DISCUSSION QUESTIONS

1. Explain the upward slopes of the IB and EB curves in the Mundell-Fleming diagram. Why is the IB curve steeper than the EB curve?

2. Discuss the need to use two instruments to simultaneously attainment of two targets. Why is it more efficient to assign the monetary policy instrument to pursue EB and the fiscal policy instruments to pursue IB targets?

3. Discuss the derivation and the slope of the LM curve.

4. Discuss the derivation and the slope of the IS curve.

5. The BP curve is constructed under the assumption of a fixed exchange rate. Discuss the potential impact of changes in the exchange rate, foreign price level, and foreign wealth on the BP curve.

6. Explain the relationship between the slope of the BP curve and international capital mobility.

7. In the case of perfect capital mobility, compare and contrast the impact of expansionary fiscal and monetary policy.

8. In the case of perfectly immobile capital, compare and contrast the impact of contractionary fiscal and monetary policy.

9. Discuss the impact of an appreciation of the home currency under the assumption of imperfect capital mobility. Do changes in the capital mobility assumption impact the result? Why or why not?

PROBLEMS

1. Using the Mundell-Fleming diagram in Figure 1 (p. 579), identify the conditions reflected by the missed targets associated with each of the following points:

    a) a

    b) b

    c) c

    d) d

2. Using the IS/LM/BP model, designate the curve and the direction of the shift from the following shocks to the economy:

    a) increase in the money supply

b) decrease in government expenditure

c) appreciation of the home currency

d) increase in taxes

e) increase in foreign income

CASE STUDY QUESTIONS
Refer to Case Study #1 (p. 591) The Presence of Exchange Controls in the Current Financial System

1. What does the information in Table 1 suggest about the international capital mobility assumptions made in the IS/LM/BP model?

2. Discuss the impact of payment restrictions in B.1. and B.2. of Table 1. Why would nations be more likely to restrict capital transactions?

3. What characteristics do the nations identified as having relatively mobile capital share? What does this suggest about the characteristics of the nations using these restrictions?

Refer to Case Study #2 (p. 599) Interdependent Monetary Policies Under Fixed Exchange Rates: The European Community

1. If the major nations of the European Union have floating exchange rates, why is their experience similar to a pegged exchange rate system?

2. What were the reasons that the non-German members of the European Union could not successfully address the slow growth of the 1980s with expansionary fiscal policy?

3. What difficulties prevented the use of discretionary fiscal policy to address the slowdown in economic activity?

4. Why was the range of movement within the ERM expanded from 2.25 percent to 15 percent?

5. Does this adjustment bode well for the European desire to achieve the status of a full economic union?

ANSWERS

True/False Questions
1. False
2. True
3. True
4. False
5. True
6. True
7. True
8. False
9. False
10. True

Fill-in questions
1. inflation; BOP surplus
2. IV
3. surplus
4. money market
5. balance of payments
6. real sector
7. perfect capital immobility
8. sterilization
9. crowding out
10. ineffective

Problems
1.
   a. inflation; BOP surplus
   b. unemployment; BOP deficit
   c. inflation; BOP deficit
   d. unemployment; BOP surplus

2.
   a. shift LM to the right
   b. shift IS to the right
   c. shift BP to the left
   d. shift IS to the left
   e. increase in exports shifts BP to the right
      expansion of exports also shifts IS to the right

CHAPTER 27
Economic Policy in the Open Economy: Flexible Exchange Rates

SUMMARY

This chapter examines economic policy in the open economy with flexible exchange rates. This matches the floating exchange rate policy adopted by many major trading countries of the world in 1973. Using the IS/LM/BP model, disequilibrium in the foreign exchange market will now lead to adjustments in the exchange rate that bring the foreign exchange market back into equilibrium.

In the flexible exchange rate system, if the economy moves to a point below the BP curve the deficit pressure (an incipient deficit) results in a depreciation in the home currency. The depreciation of the home currency shifts the BP curve to the right. Analogously, a combination of income and interest rate above the BP curve causes surplus pressure (an incipient surplus) and results in an appreciation of the home currency. This currency appreciation shifts the BP curve to the left.

As in the previous chapter, the effects of fiscal and monetary policy under different capital mobility assumptions are examined. The effectiveness of fiscal policy depends strongly on the degree of international mobility of capital. When capital is completely or relatively immobile, fiscal policy is effective in moving the to income and interest rate targets. As capital becomes more mobile, fiscal policy becomes less effective. When the LM curve is steeper than BP, the expansionary fiscal policy causes an income-depressing appreciation of the home currency. In the extreme case of perfect capital mobility, fiscal policy is totally ineffective because the increase in government spending results in exports being "crowded out" by imports. The movement to a flexible exchange rate system weakens the fiscal policy instrument in a world of mobile capital.

The effectiveness of monetary policy is increased by the movement to flexible exchange rates. Increases in the money supply shift the LM curve to the right putting downward pressure on interest rates and expanding domestic income. The expansionary monetary policy results in depreciation of the home currency (rightward shifts in BP) and a rightward shift in IS as net exports increase. As the capital becomes more mobile (BP becomes flatter), the depreciation and increase in net exports get larger. The overall expansionary effects of monetary policy are larger as capital becomes more mobile.

Overall, in a system with flexible exchange rates, monetary policy becomes more effective as international short-term capital becomes more mobile. Fiscal policy is less effective when capital is relatively or perfectly mobile. Policymakers may find it desirable to use monetary policy-fiscal policy coordination to achieve domestic targets. Policymakers find it very difficult to achieve interest rate and income targets using one policy instrument without changing the relative prices and structure of the economy. A coordinated use of both policies is a superior way to achieve targets and react to shocks.

Given the need for policy coordination, an analysis of the impact of potential shocks helps determine the preferred policy reaction. An external or foreign price shock will initially shift IS and BP, but the adjustments is the exchange rate correct the resulting changes. Flexible exchange rates insulate the economy from foreign price shocks. In contrast, a domestic price shock shifts IS, BP, and LM. The adjustment ends with an equilibrium point on the new LM curve establishing a new interest rate and income level.

Foreign interest rate shocks result in shifts of both IS and BP. The new equilibrium reflects an adjustment in the domestic interest rate toward the new foreign rate and a corresponding change in income. A shock to the expected exchange rate has a similar impact as foreign interest rate shocks. While the economy corrects automatically to a new equilibrium, the interest rate and income targets may not be hit. As one considers that a variety of these shocks could occur simultaneously, finding the appropriate combination of policies becomes much more difficult. An attempt to counter this difficulty is seen in attempts to have international macroeconomic policy coordination.

DEFINE THE FOLLOWING KEY TERMS

domestic price shock (p. 614)

foreign interest rate shock (p. 615)

foreign price shock (p. 613)

G-7 countries (p. 617)

incipient deficit (p. 604)

incipient surplus (p. 604)

international macroeconomic policy coordination (p. 617)

monetary policy-fiscal policy coordination (p. 611)

shock to the expected exchange rate (p. 616)

TRUE/FALSE QUESTIONS

1. Under a fixed exchange rate system, fiscal policy was ineffective, but with flexible exchange rates fiscal policy is effective in all cases except when capital is perfectly immobile.

2. Under a system of flexible exchange rates, an appreciation of the home currency is represented by a leftward shift of the BP curve.

3. An incipient deficit triggers a depreciation of the home currency and a shift of the BP curve to the right.

4. An increase in foreign income and an increase in foreign prices result in shifts of the BP curve to the right.

5. Under a flexible exchange rate system, fiscal policy is effective when capital is perfectly immobile and ineffective when capital is perfectly mobile.

6. Under a flexible exchange rate system, as capital becomes more mobile the expansionary effects of increased government spending is complemented by an improvement in the current account that accompanies the appreciation of the currency.

7. Under a system of flexible exchange rates, expansionary monetary policy leads to an appreciation of the currency, accompanied by an increase in imports and a decrease in exports.

8. The only way to simultaneously achieve income and interest rate targets without causing exchange rate changes is to rely on both fiscal and monetary policy instruments.

9. A foreign price shock that causes exports to increase and imports to decrease would shift both the LM and the BP to the right.

10. A foreign interest rate shock will tend to push the domestic interest rate in the same direction as the shock.

FILL-IN QUESTIONS

1. Since 1973, many major trading countries have stopped pegging their currencies and have let their currencies _____.

2. An increase in domestic prices would tend to shift the BP curve to the _____, while an increase in foreign prices would tend to shift the BP curve to the _____.

3. Under a system of fixed exchange rates, monetary policy is (effective/ineffective) while with flexible exchange rates monetary policy is (effective/ineffective).

4. The need to use two policy instruments to achieve two policy targets requires _____.

5. A sudden increase in domestic prices is known as a _____.

6. An increase in the foreign interest rate is referred to as a _____.

7. A foreign price shock would be a sudden increase or decrease in _____ prices.

8. The _____ consists of the US, Canada, France, Germany, Italy, Japan, and the U.K.

9. An expectation of a greater appreciation of a foreign currency as a result of a foreign election would be considered a _____.

10. The _____ is seen as a means to reduce the degree of instability of exchange rates and domestic variables.

DISCUSSION QUESTIONS

1. Explain an incipient surplus and the changes in exchange rate and BP curve as a result of its existence.

2. Assume an IS/LM/BP model with flexible exchange rates. The BP curve is steeper than the LM curve. Discuss the relative effectiveness of expansionary fiscal and monetary policy.

3. Assume an IS/LM/BP model with flexible exchange rates. The LM curve is steeper than the BP curve. Discuss the relative effectiveness of contractionary fiscal and monetary policy.

4. Assume that the BP curve is perfectly inelastic and exchange rates are flexible. Choose and defend a policy to increase the level of domestic income.

5. Assume that the BP curve is perfectly elastic and exchange rates are flexible. Choose and defend a policy to decrease the level of domestic income.

6. Discuss the need for monetary policy-fiscal policy coordination to simultaneously achieve two targets without impacting exchange rates.

7. Explain the insulation of the economy from foreign price shocks under a system of flexible exchange rates.

8. Discuss the changes that result from a decrease in the foreign interest rate under a system of flexible exchange rates.

PROBLEMS

1. Identify the appropriate shift in the BP curve as a result of the following changes in exogenous factors:

    a. decrease in foreign income

    b. increase in foreign interest rate

    c. increase in expected domestic profits

    d. decrease in domestic prices

    e. increase in expected home country currency depreciation

    f. decrease in expected foreign profits

CASE STUDY QUESTIONS

Refer to Case Study 1 (p. 614) Commodity Prices and U.S. Real GDP, 1973-1995

1. With the exception of petroleum, what has the trend in commodity prices been from the mid-1970's through the mid-1980s?

2. Given perfectly flexible exchange rates, what would be the impact of the oil price shock in 1973-74? What actually happened in the U.S. economy?

3. Would a shock in nonfuel primary commodities (similar to the 1973 petroleum shock) have the same impact on the U.S. economy? Why or why not?

Refer to Case Study 2 (p. 618) Macroeconomic Policy Coordination, the IMF, and the G-7

1. Why has international macroeconomic policy coordination become a major objective of industrial countries?

2. The G-7 nations appear to be working toward greater international policy coordination. Are there other examples of nations seeking greater coordination of policies and goals?

3. What targets seem to be most important from the standpoint of international policy coordination?

4. List and explain the problems associated with the movement toward greater international macroeconomic policy coordination.

ANSWERS

True/False Questions
1. False
2. True
3. True
4. True
5. True
6. False
7. False
8. True
9. False
10. True

Fill-in questions
1. float
2. left; right
3. ineffective; effective
4. monetary policy - fiscal policy coordination
5. domestic price shock
6. foreign interest rate shock
7. foreign
8. G-7 countries or Group of 7
9. shock to the expected exchange rate
10. international macroeconomic policy coordination

Problems
1. a. BP shifts to the left
   b. BP shifts to the left
   c. BP shifts to the right
   d. BP shifts to the right
   e. BP shifts to the left
   f. BP shifts to the right

CHAPTER 28
Prices and Output in the Open Economy: Aggregate Supply and Demand

SUMMARY

This chapter takes an additional step in the analysis of fiscal and monetary policy in the open economy. The impact of changes in the price level are examined with a movement to an aggregate supply/aggregate demand framework. The model uses a standard downward sloping aggregate demand curve which shows the level of real output demanded at each price level. In terms of aggregate supply, the time frame becomes very important. Under the assumption that labor takes some time to adjust wage demands to higher prices, the short run aggregate supply curve is upward sloping. Given time for labor to react, increases in the price level will not impact the level of real output. As a result, the long-run aggregate supply curve is vertical at the natural level of income.

Equilibrium in the aggregate supply/aggregate demand framework occurs where all three curves (AS_{LR}, AS_{SR}, AD) intersect. Moving from the closed economy to an open economy primarily impacts aggregate demand (i.e. adding imports and exports). The analysis that follows assumes that capital is imperfectly immobile between countries and that the BP curve is flatter than the LM curve. The effects of changes in aggregate demand and aggregate supply in the open economy will be examined with fixed exchange rates and flexible exchange rates.

The derivation of an aggregate demand curve for an open economy requires the examination of the impact of rising prices on real output. Under fixed exchange rates, rising prices leads to an expenditure-switching effect that makes aggregate demand more elastic in the open economy compared to the closed economy. With flexible exchange rates, increases in prices still lead to decreases in real income resulting in the normal downward-sloping aggregate demand curve. If imports and exports are price inelastic, the flexible rate AD is more elastic than the fixed rate AD. If imports and exports are price elastic the fixed rate AD is more elastic than the flexible rate AD.

Shocks that impact IS, LM, or BP can have an impact on AD. The direction and magnitude of the impact may depend on the existence of fixed or flexible exchange rates. In the case of an increase in foreign interest rates, the AD curve will shift to the left with fixed exchange rates. With flexible rates, the home currency depreciation results in a rightward shift in AD. Similarly, a shift in preferences toward home investments will prove to be expansionary under fixed rates, but the appreciation of the currency that occurs with flexible rates leads to a decrease in income and aggregate demand.

The impacts of fiscal and monetary policy will be governed by the type of exchange rate system and the imperfect capital mobility assumption. Under a fixed exchange rate system, monetary policy was ineffective in influencing AD while fiscal policy proved very effective. The movement to a system of flexible exchange rate results in a major change. With greater capital mobility, monetary policy is much more effective in impacting AD. Given the current capital mobility assumption, fiscal policy is relatively ineffective.

An examination of monetary policy is the AS/AD framework results in two different outcomes. If exchange rates are fixed, monetary policy has no impact on AD and can be ignored. If exchange rates are flexible, expansionary monetary policy increases AD (shifts it to the right). The result is a short-run increase in income and employment, but it will only last until workers adjust their wage demands to the new higher level of prices. The rising prices will have an impact on nominal interest rates and the exchange rate. If the economy is below full employment, expansionary monetary policy can be used to stimulate the economy but at the expense of higher prices.

In the case of fiscal policy, the results are very similar to those in the case of monetary policy. Under flexible exchange rates, fiscal policy is relatively ineffective unless capital is relatively immobile. With fixed exchange rates, the income and employment stimulus of expansionary fiscal policy are only temporary. Once labor adjusts its wage demands, the economy returns to the natural level of income and employment. Only the inflation remains. The effectiveness of either fiscal or monetary policy in the short run depends on a certain degree of inflexibility of wages and prices. If prices and wages are flexible, the market can correct movements from full employment without the inflationary impact of the policy actions. For discretionary policy to have any long-term impact, it must contribute to growing productive capacity (shift AS_{LR} to the right).

The final concern is the impact of external shocks within the open economy with flexible prices. An increase in the world price of an intermediate input results in a decrease in AS (leftward shift of AS_{SR} and AS_{LR}). The declining income combined with inflation is known as stagflation. An inflow of short-term capital would decrease AD. Expansionary monetary policy or adjustments by labor to the lower price level are needed to return the economy to its initial equilibrium. An improvement in aggregate productivity will shift the AS_{SR} and AS_{LR} curves to the right. Expansionary monetary policy or decreases in wages are necessary to bring the system back to short-run and long-run equilibrium. Once again, the choice between the discretionary policy move and the market alternative depends on the assumptions related to adjustments in prices and wages.

DEFINE THE FOLLOWING KEY TERMS
aggregate demand curve (p. 622)

aggregate demand curve for labor (p. 624)

aggregate production function (p. 623)

aggregate supply-aggregate demand equilibrium (p. 628)

contractionary devaluation (p. 638)

Fisher effect (p. 636)

international Fisher effect (p. 636)

long-run aggregate supply curve (p. 626)

natural level of employment (p. 626)

natural level of income (p. 626)

short-run aggregate supply curve (p. 624)

short-run aggregate supply curve of labor (p. 625)

stagflation (p. 641)

TRUE/FALSE QUESTIONS

1. An aggregate production function is used to represent the relationship between price and output.

2. Under the assumption of rational expectations, the short run aggregate supply curve would be non-vertical representing the response of output to prices.

3. Aggregate supply-aggregate demand equilibrium occurs where AS_{LR}, AS_{SR}, and AD all intersect.

4. The stronger the expenditure-switching effect in an open economy with fixed exchange rates, the steeper the aggregate demand curve is in the open economy compared to the closed economy.

5. In an open economy with flexible prices, an increase in the foreign interest rate will lead to a leftward shift of AD if the exchange rate is fixed and a rightward shift if the exchange rate is flexible.

6. If exchange rates are flexible, monetary policy has no effect on AD but fiscal policy is effective when capital is perfectly mobile internationally.

7. If exchange rates are fixed, expansionary fiscal policy can stimulate income and employment in the short run, but only temporarily.

8. If discretionary fiscal or monetary policy is to have any lasting effect other than to increase prices, the increase in AD must not be offset by a corresponding decrease in AS_{LR}.

9. An improvement in aggregate productivity due to a change in technology shifts the AS_{SR} and AS_{LR} to the right.

10. In general, the greater the increase in wages necessary to attract the additional labor, the steeper the short run aggregate supply curve of labor.

FILL-IN QUESTIONS

1. The _____ curve shows the level of real output demanded at each price level.

2. Multiplying the MPP_N by the level of prices produces the _____ curve.

3. The _____ is the level of employment at which the actual price level equals the expected price level by workers.

4. The _____ aggregate supply curve is vertical at the natural level of income.

5. Under flexible exchange rates, expansionary monetary policy shifts the AD curve to the _____.

6. Under fixed exchange rates, a change in foreign tastes that decreases home country exports shifts the AD curve to the _____.

7. The _____ argues that the percentage change in the relative nominal interest rates between two countries should equal the expected percentage change in the exchange rate.

8. When intermediate imports are very important to a developing country, if a decrease in AS_{SR} and AS_{LR} resulting from a devaluation cause output to fall, this is known as a _____.

9. Declining income coupled with rising inflation is often referred to as _____.

10. The _____ suggests that any difference in the nominal rates of interest must be attributable to differences in the expected inflation rate in the two countries.

DISCUSSION QUESTIONS
1. Discuss the use of the IS/LM model with flexible prices to derive an aggregate demand curve.

2. Discuss the assumptions that result in a nonvertical short-run aggregate supply curve.

3. Explain the relationships between the natural level of employment, the natural level of income, and the long-run aggregate supply curve.

4. Explain why the expenditure-switching effect results in an aggregate demand curve that is flatter in the open economy relative to a closed economy when exchange rates are fixed.

5. Assume a decrease in the foreign interest rate. Discuss the impact on AD when exchange rates are fixed. Does the outcome differ if exchange rates are flexible? Why or why not?

6. Given a fixed exchange rate system, discuss the impacts of fiscal and monetary policy on AD.

7. Given a flexible exchange rate system, discuss the impacts of fiscal and monetary policy on AD.

8. Compare and contrast the impacts of an increase in the price of an intermediate input and an improvement in aggregate productivity using an AS/AD model.

PROBLEMS
1. Using Figure 9 on page 635, identify the following:
   a. the initial equilibrium price and income

   b. short run equilibrium price and quantity

   c. new equilibrium after wage rates adjust to the price increases.

   d. what is the long-run impact of the expansionary monetary policy?

2. Under a fixed exchange rate system, identify the impact of each change on AD.
   a. contractionary monetary policy

   b. expansionary fiscal policy

   c. change in taste that reduces home country exports

   d. interest rate change that stimulates short-term capital outflow

3. Under a flexible exchange rate system, identify the impact of each change on AD.
   a. expansionary monetary policy

   b. contractionary fiscal policy

   c. change in foreign tastes that increase home country exports

   d. change in foreign interest rate that results in an outflow of short-term capital from the home country.

CASE STUDY QUESTIONS
Refer to Case Study 1 (p. 627) U.S. Actual and Natural Income, Employment, and Unemployment

1. Discuss the conditions in the economy when the Actual Real GDP exceeds the Natural Real GDP.

2. What is true of the economy when the Actual Employment is less than the Natural Employment?

3. Discuss the use of fiscal and monetary policy to address the problems of the economy from 1981-1986? Would the policies be the same for the period 1965-1970? Why or why not?

Refer to Case Study 2 (p. 642) Inflation and Unemployment in the U.S. 1970-1996

1. The term stagflation is often used to describe the periods from 1973-1975 and 1979-1981. Use the data from this case to explain that designation.

2. From 1982 on, the inflation rate has been below the unemployment rate. What type of monetary policy would you associate with this period? Why?

3. If the natural rate of unemployment is 6%, what years between 1970 and 1996 would have raised concerns for policymakers? What policies would be considered to address these concerns? Why?

ANSWERS

True/False Questions
1. False
2. False
3. True
4. False
5. True
6. False
7. True
8. False
9. True
10. True

Fill-in questions
1. aggregate demand
2. marginal revenue product
3. natural level of employment
4. long run
5. right
6. left
7. international Fischer effect
8. contractionary devaluation
9. stagflation
10. Fischer effect

Problems
1. a. P_0; Y_0
   b. P_1; Y_1
   c. P_2; Y_0
   d. an increase in prices from P_0 to P_2 with no corresponding increase in real income.

2. a. no impact on AD
   b. shifts AD right
   c. shifts AD left
   d. shifts AD left

3. a. shifts AD right
   b. little effect on AD (slight leftward shift possible)
   c. no effect on AD
   d. shifts AD right

CHAPTER 29
Fixed or Flexible Exchange Rates?

SUMMARY

This chapter focuses on the debate over the degree of exchange rate stability that should be permitted. In that debate, the term fixed exchange rate refers to a system that permits only very small, if any, deviations from officially declared currency values. Flexible exchange rates refer to rates that are completely free to vary, that is, the foreign exchange market is cleared at all times by changes in the exchange rate. The debate will assess the two extremes and potential "middle ground" solutions.

The analysis will compare the two exchange rate systems in terms of six critical questions. The first question addressed relates to the discipline placed on policymakers to prevent continuing inflation. Advocates of a fixed exchange rate system believe that the system does have anti-inflation discipline because BOP deficits result in deflation and BOP surpluses cause inflation. With price flexibility in each country, it is likely that world prices will be relatively stable. Flexible rates are believed to aggravate inflationary tendencies in a country because inflation leads to depreciation of a currency which adds to aggregate demand and inflationary pressure. The proponents of flexible rates believe that inflation signals the need for monetary restraint and that the danger of inflation is therefore no greater. The discipline of fixed rates may also be undesirable. The automatic adjustment to control inflation may force other domestic goals to be sacrificed or delayed. The question of the prevalence of greater discipline in one system must be settled by empirical research.

The second question is related to growth in international trade and investment. Proponents of a fixed rate system focus on the risk and uncertainty associated with flexible rates. They argue that exports and foreign investments are reduced as a result of the risk of exchange rate changes. Advocates of flexible rates would focus on the ability to hedge in the forward market, the potential for increased DFI to avoid currency fluctuations, and the negative impact of sterilization by nations under fixed rate systems on efficient resource allocation. This question is difficult to answer because a country cannot be tested in a laboratory environment.

The third question is related to efficiency of resource allocation. Advocates of flexible rates believe that fixing any price will lead to a misallocation of resources because prices are not allowed to reflect true scarcity values. Fixing exchange rates also requires a portion of the nation's capital be tied up as international reserves. Advocates of fixed rates believe that changes in exchange rates result in unnecessary and wasteful resource movements. Fixed rates will avoid these unwarranted movements. Overall, there does appear to be an opportunity cost associated with foregone capital stock and output due to the reserve holding under fixed rates.

The fourth question is related to the effectiveness of macroeconomic policy. This portion of the debate is clouded by different preferences associated with the proper role of government, direct versus indirect government influence, and fiscal versus monetary policy. The issue is truly debatable only when fiscal policy is preferred to monetary policy as the instrument of choice.

Fiscal policy is more effective in influencing the level of national income under fixed rates than under flexible rates. In defense of flexible rates, monetary policy and the exchange rate are additional tools that are part of the nation's policy arsenal. The attainment of multiple targets often requires that the number of instruments matches the number of targets. Policy preferences, and therefore exchange rate policies of choice, will vary from country to country.

The fifth question is related to the presence of destabilizing speculation. Those opposed to flexible exchange rates believe that normal economic fluctuations will be augmented by destabilizing speculation. The speculation occurs but there is substantial debate over whether it is destabilizing and whether it is a result of flexible exchange rates. Fixed exchange rate systems can also result in destabilizing speculation. This is important because the presence of destabilizing speculation could make it unlikely that a fixed rate system can operate successfully.

The sixth question relates to protection from external shocks. In the case of external <u>real</u> sector shocks the fixed exchange rate system contributes to the transmission of business cycles from one nation to another. In a flexible rate situation, the exchange rate would mitigate the transmission. If the external shock is a financial sector shock, neither exchange rate will "insulate" the economy from the shock but their impacts on income will be in opposite directions.

The concept of an optimum currency area is an attempt to design the combination of fixed and flexible rates that are optimal for BOP adjustments and policy effectiveness. The suggestion is that rates should be fixed within the area but flexible to outside trading partners. McKinnon's analysis took the debate one step further suggesting that relatively open economies should consider fixed rates while relatively closed economies should adopt flexible exchange rates.

Given the uncertainty associated with the fixed versus flexible rates debate, several hybrid proposals have emerged. The proposals include fixed rates with a wide band of flexibility to account for BOP adjustments with limited exchange rate variability. An exchange rate that fluctuates within a narrow band with the possibility of small depreciations or depreciations as necessary is known as a crawling peg. An adjustment to flexible exchange rate systems to allow some interference in exchange rate movements is known as a managed float. In some cases the intervention involves a coordinated effort among several nations. There is also a danger of abuse. Some nations may try to contrive comparative advantage by exchange rate protection. Others use managed floats in order to pursue particular goals at the expense of other countries in a behavior known as dirty floating.

DEFINE THE FOLLOWING KEY TERMS
coordinated intervention (p. 666)

crawling peg (p. 665)

destabilizing speculation (p. 657)

dirty floating (p. 668)

exchange rate protection (p. 668)

"leaning against the wind" (p. 666)

"leaning with the wind" (p. 666)

managed floating (p. 666)

optimal size of international reserves (p. 654)

optimum currency area (p. 577)

precautionary demand for international reserves (p. 654)

stabilizing speculation (p. 658)

transactions demand for international reserves (p. 654)

vicious circle hypothesis (p. 650)

wider bands (p. 664)

TRUE/FALSE QUESTIONS

1. The discipline of a fixed rate system suggests that there should be no tendency for greater inflation to occur in one country than in the world as a whole.

2. In a fixed exchange rate system, if a country has a BOP surplus, deflation will result in order to offset the surplus.

3. A flexible exchange rate system is thought to bring with it a considerable amount of risk and uncertainty potentially impacting direct foreign investment.

4. Proponents of flexible rates believe the absence of a flexible price for foreign exchange in a fixed-rate system generates widespread price distortions and gives misleading signals.

5. The demand for international reserves by nations can be divided into two components: transactions demand and speculative demand.

6. The international reserves necessary in a fixed exchange rate system have an opportunity cost of foregone capital stock and the foregone output that capital could have produced.

7. The fact that destabilizing speculation cannot occur under a fixed exchange rate system is a strong argument against flexible rates.

8. An important argument for a fixed exchange rate system is that, in such a system, business cycles cannot be transmitted from one country to another.

9. In the context of the fixed rate-flexible rate debate, McKinnon suggested that relatively open economies should consider flexible rates, while relatively closed economies should adopt fixed rates.

10. In a managed float, there is a danger of abuse to the free allocation of resources according to comparative advantage if countries engage in exchange rate protection.

FILL-IN QUESTIONS

1. The manipulation of managed floats to pursue goals at the expense of other countries is referred to as _____.

2. A country that intervenes in order to slow down a movement in the exchange rate in a particular direction is said to be _____.

3. A _____ is a system in which a country specifies a parity value for its currency and permits a small variation around that parity.

4. An _____ area has fixed exchange rates within the area but flexible exchange rates with trading partners outside the area.

5. A situation in which normal fluctuations that occur with flexible rates are augmented by the behavior of speculators attempting to make profits on the basic anticipations of future exchange rates is _____.

6. Extra international reserves held by a country in order to guard against unexpected negative developments in the balance of payments is known as the _____.

7. The _____ hypothesis argues that under flexible rates inflation in a country is aggravated by depreciation in the exchange market and becomes self-perpetuating.

8. Proponents of _____ rate attack _____ rate systems because of its key characteristic that fixes the most important price in the economy.

9. Fiscal policy is more effective in influencing the level of national income under _____ rates than under _____ rates.

10. With limited international reserves, slow adjustment, and destabilizing speculation, deficit countries will ultimately have to devalue and the _____ system will break down.

DISCUSSION QUESTIONS

1. Discuss the concept of "discipline" in economic policy. Explain why fixed rates are thought to bring more policy discipline than flexible rates.

2. Explain the role of risk and uncertainty in the debate over the impact of exchange rate policy on growth in trade and investment.

3. Given a nation prefers to use fiscal policy rather than monetary policy. Discuss the impact of fixed and flexible exchange rates on the effectiveness of the policy actions.

4. If a nation prefers to use monetary policy to achieve economic goals, would a fixed rate system be preferred to a flexible rate system? Why or why not?

5. Define destabilizing speculation. Discuss the possibility of this type of speculation in a fixed exchange rate system.

6. Discuss the differences between real and nominal shocks in an attempt to analyze the impact of the exchange rate system on protecting a nation from external shocks.

7. Define an optimal currency area. Compare and contrast the suggestions of Mundell and McKinnon.

8. Assume a managed floating regime. Explain the difference between coordinated intervention and a dirty float.

CASE STUDY QUESTIONS
Refer to Case Study 1 (p. 653) Exchange Risk and International Trade

1. How are risks associated with exchange rates thought to impact international trade and development?

2. Given that the Thursby's and Cushman found negative relationships between the size of trade and nominal rate variability, which exchange rate system would be preferable? Why?

3. The impact of risk and uncertainty on direct foreign investment is also an issue. How would you set up an empirical analysis to address the impact of flexible exchange rates on DFI?

Refer to Case Study 2 (P. 655) Reserve Holdings Under Fixed and Flexible Exchange Rates

1. Why do nations find it necessary to hold international reserves under a fixed exchange rate system?

2. What happened to the absolute opportunity cost of holding international reserves after 1973? What happened to the relative opportunity cost of holding international reserves.

3. For 1996, what would happen to the opportunity cost of holding international reserves if the nations went back to the Bretton Woods ratio of reserves to imports.

4. Is the magnitude of the reserves after 1973 an indication of a managed float regime? Why or why not?

Refer to Case Study 3 (p. 662) "Insulation" with Flexible Rates: The Case of Japan

1. What is meant by "insulation" of an economy from external shocks?

2. Why are the two exchange rate systems expected to have differences in their ability to insulate an economy?

3. How are Hutchison and Walsh able to overcome the problems associated with the relative size of external shocks.

4. What aspects of the Hutchison and Walsh results were as expected? Which results were somewhat surprising?

Refer to Case Study 4 (p. 667) A Crawling Peg in Columbia

1. What is a crawling peg exchange rate system? What factors are considered in making the adjustments?

2. Does the choice of currency for Columbia's peg have an impact on the "crawling" process? Why?

3. What is the expected impact of a devaluation of this magnitude on a nation's international trade?

4. Do these results suggest that Columbia should have maintained a more rigid system of fixed exchange rates? Why or why not?

ANSWERS

True/False Questions
1. True
2. False
3. True
4. True
5. False
6. True
7. False
8. False
9. False
10. True

Fill-in questions
1. dirty floating
2. leaning against the wind
3. crawling peg
4. optimal currency
5. destabilizing speculation
6. precautionary demand for international reserves
7. vicious circle
8. flexible; fixed
9. fixed; flexible
10. fixed rate

CHAPTER 30
The International Monetary System: Past, Present, and Future

SUMMARY

The choice of an international monetary system involves efficient BOP adjustment, international liquidity, internationally accepted reserve assets, and confidence in the assets. This chapter examines the history of international monetary systems and some suggestions for improvements in the future. From 1880 until 1914 the prevailing system was an international gold standard. The system contributed to relatively free trade and payments but broke down when WWI began. A variety of attempts were made to institute a new system following the war. In 1944, the Bretton Woods system emerged and was supported by the formation of the International Monetary Fund (IMF) and the World Bank. The Bretton Woods system called for pegged but adjustable exchange rates. The system sought to obtain exchange rate stability, reconcile country adjustments to payments imbalances with national policy autonomy, and help preserve relatively free trade and payments in the world economy. The Bretton Woods system served well until the mid-1960s and then fell victim to liquidity problems, confidence problems, and adjustment problems.

A variety of events have contributed to the development of the current international monetary system. The IMF developed a new international asset known as special drawing rights (SDRs) for quota accounting and BOP assistance loans. The SDRs became especially important in 1971 when the U.S. announced that it would no longer buy and sell gold. The fall of the "gold guarantee" led to the Smithsonian agreement which instituted greater exchange rate flexibility. The Jamaica Accords in 1976 allowed IMF member countries to choose their own exchange rate arrangement. The European Community responded in 1979 by establishing the European Monetary System (EMS) which developed a new currency, the ecu, and set a small range of adjustment for currencies of EC nations. The EMS took a major step on the road toward full economic integration in 1991 with the signing of the Maastricht Treaty. The European Union's progress toward full monetary integration has been problematic, but recent actions suggest that qualification criteria will be relaxed in order to lock currencies in 1999. The movement from Bretton Woods to the current system of floating exchange rates has resulted in a substantial increase in exchange rate fluctuations.

The current international monetary system is actually a conglomerate of systems. While the trend has been toward greater freedom to float a variety of pegging systems still exist. The experience since Bretton woods has been characterized by greater variability, overshooting, real economic effects of the variability, lack of insulation from external shocks, and the need to hold larger than expected shocks of international reserves. The characteristic that is missing is the increase in inflation that was predicted to come with greater flexibility.

With the variety of choices in the current system comes a group of suggestions for reforming the international monetary system. Most of the proposals are designed to decrease the current level of exchange rate volatility. The list of proposals includes the return to the gold standard, establishing a world central bank, setting targets for real effective exchange rates, establishing controls on capital flows, and increasing the coordination of macroeconomic policies across countries. While each proposal has its advocates, there is no indication that a new international system will be adopted. The trend does seem to be toward greater policy coordination among groups of nations but a formal arrangement is perceived as a challenge to a nation's sovereignty.

Developing nations seem to prefer fixed exchange rates due to the high ratio of trade to GDP and exchange rate volatility. LDCs would like a system that enhances the development prospects, has fewer restrictions associated with international borrowing, and generates more stability in the world economy. In an attempt to support development efforts many developing countries turned to banks in developed nations. The extent of this borrowing led to the LDC debt "crisis."

In the 1970's, the external debt of LDCs grew very rapidly. While developing nations in all areas have generated external debt, the nations of Latin America, the Caribbean, and Africa have the most severe problems. The factors that have played a causal role in the LDC debt problem include oil price increases, recessions in the industrialized nations, rising interest rates, falling prices of primary products, poor domestic policies, capital flight, and "loan pushing" by banks in developed countries. The debt crisis created problems for developing countries, but also disrupted the financial sector in developed countries. A variety of policies were used to help these nations through their debt problems.

The key to successful policies was the realization that the problem was long-term solvency rather than a short-term liquidity problem. The solutions included debt rescheduling, debt relief, and debt equity swaps to reduce the amount of outstanding debt and the magnitude of the payments. In addition, the IMF and the World Bank focused on structural adjustment policies in order to strengthen each nation's long-term repayment prospects.

DEFINE THE FOLLOWING KEY TERMS
adequacy of reserves problem (liquidity problem) (p. 675)

adjustment problem (p. 677)

balance-of-payments adjustment mechanism (p. 671)

Brady Plan (p. 708)

Bretton Woods system (p. 674)

confidence problem (p. 677)

convergency criteria (p. 682)

credit tranche (p. 675)

debt-equity swaps (p. 711)

debt relief or debt reduction (p. 708)

debt-relief Laffer curve (p. 708-709)

debt rescheduling (p. 708)

debt service ratio (p. 705)

dual exchange rates or multiple exchange rates (p. 700)

Economic and Monetary Union (EMU) (p. 681)

euro (p. 682)

European Currency Unit or ecu (p. 681)

European Monetary Cooperation Fund (EMCF) (p. 681)

European Monetary System (EMS) (p. 681)

European System of Central Banks (ESCB) (p. 682)

Exchange Rate Mechanism (ERM) (p. 681)

gold tranche or reserve tranche (p. 675)

IMF conditionality (p. 703)

IMF quota (p. 675)

international liquidity (p. 671)

International Monetary Fund (IMF) (p. 674)

internationally acceptable reserve assets (p. 671)

Jamaica Accords (p. 680)

key currencies (p. 678)

link proposal (p. 703)

Maastricht Treaty (p. 681)

pegged but adjustable exchange rates (p. 674)

secondary debt market (p. 709)

Smithsonian Agreement (p. 680)

special drawing rights (SDRs) (p. 678)

structural adjustment policies (p. 707)

surveillance (p. 680)

target zone proposal (p. 696)

transfer problem (p. 705)

TRUE/FALSE QUESTIONS

1. Completely flexible exchange rates are characterized by the need for an internationally acceptable reserve asset and an adequate supply of international liquidity.

2. The gold tranche referred to the 75 percent of the IMF reserve quota that must be held as gold.

3. When introduced in 1970, special drawing rights were valued at 1/35 of an ounce of gold equal to the value of one U.S. dollar.

4. The Smithsonian Agreement in 1971 allowed each IMF member country to adopt its own exchange rate arrangements.

5. The Maastricht Treaty set out a plan for a European central bank and a common currency by January 1, 1999.

6. Most nations that currently have a pegged exchange rate, peg the value of their currency to the SDR.

7. While the nominal exchange rates have fluctuated rapidly since the end of the Bretton Woods system, the variability has had no real economic effects.

8. An extreme form of the proposal for a world central bank suggests the use of a single world currency as the means of controlling the money supply.

9. IMF conditionality refers to the requirement that nations put up gold as collateral as a condition for receiving loans.

10. The debt-relief Laffer curve implies that the market value of a nation's debt can become such a burden that the face value actually falls below the market value.

FILL-IN QUESTIONS

1. The International Monetary Fund (IMF) was the key institution in the functioning of the international monetary system known as the _____ system.

2. All Nations joining the IMF were assigned a quota paid in gold and the nation's currency. Countries can obtain loans against the quota with the first 25 percent borrowed known as the _____.

3. The three major problems that eventually led to the end of the Bretton Woods system were a _____ problem, the _____ problem, and the _____ problem.

4. The national currencies most prominently held by central banks as official international reserves are known as _____.

5. Beginning in 1970, a new international asset known as _____ was created by the IMF and became the primary asset used when nations "borrow" from the IMF to offset short-term BOP problems.

6. The European Monetary System (EMS) created a new monetary unit, the _____.

7. The establishment of a common European currency and a European central bank by January 1, 1999 was laid out in the _____.

8. A plan by which major industrialized nations would negotiate a set of mutually consistent targets for their real effective exchange rates to reduce conflict between internal and external goals is known as the _____ proposal.

9. A system of _____ exchange rates employs a different exchange rate depending on the nature of the foreign transaction.

10. The percentage of annual export earnings that must be set aside for payment of interest on the debt and the scheduled repayment of the debt itself is the _____.

11. LDC debt instruments are bought and sold in a _____ after the initial issuance if a holder wants to exchange the bonds for other assets.

12. In a _____, a holder of a debt claim on a developing country exchanges the claim for local LDC currency which is then used to acquire shares in a productive enterprise within the LDC.

DISCUSSION QUESTIONS
1. Outline the goals of the Bretton Woods system and explain the reason the system disintegrated in the early 1970s.

2. Discuss the use of SDRs to replace gold as the asset of IMF quota valuation. Do SDRs serve as money? Why or why not?

3. Discuss the development of the European Monetary System and the changes associated with the adoption of the Maastricht treaty.

4. Discuss the performance of the post Bretton Woods experience with flexible exchange rates. Have the problems predicted by advocates of fixed rates appeared? Explain.

5. Discuss the proposals for changes to increase the stability of the exchange rate market. Describe aspects of these proposals that are currently used.

6. Explain the origin and causes of the debt crisis in developing nations.

7. Discuss the policies used to assist nations in overcoming the debt crisis. Use the debt relief Laffer curve to explain when debt relief makes financial sense.

CASE STUDY QUESTIONS

Refer to Case Study 1 (p. 672) Flexible Exchange Rates in Post-WWI Europe: The United Kingdom, France, and Norway

1. Was the expectation that a flexible exchange rate system results in considerable instability of the exchange rate evident in these 3 countries? Explain.

2. Discuss the relationship between government policy actions and the volatility of the exchange rate.

3. Do the results of flexible exchange rates from 1919-1924 suggest the need for fixed rates to maintain discipline on government policy? Why or why not?

4. Would a similar charting of the experience of western nations from 1970-1990 demonstrate a similar experience? What factors are different today?

Refer to Case Study 2 (p. 695) Estonia's Currency Board

1. What type of exchange rate system has Estonia chosen? Why would it be so classified?

2. Does this type of system facilitate the use of fiscal or monetary policy? What assumptions about capital mobility impact your answer?

3. Other transitional nations are continuing to experience negative GDP growth and rising unemployment. How will Estonia address these concerns if the problem continues to get worse?

4. Why did Estonia choose the German deutschmark instead of the Russian ruble for its peg? Was this an appropriate choice?

ANSWERS

True/False Questions
1. False
2. False
3. True
4. False
5. True
6. False
7. False
8. True
9. False
10. False

Fill-in questions
1. Bretton Woods
2. gold tranche or reserve tranche
3. liquidity; confidence; adjustment
4. key currencies
5. special drawing rights
6. European Currency Unit, ecu
7. Maastricht Treaty
8. target zone
9. dual or multiple
10. debt service ratio
11. secondary debt market
12. debt-equity swap

Study Guide
to accompany
International Economics

Third Edition

Dennis R. Appleyard
Davidson College

Alfred J. Field, Jr.
University of North Carolina

Prepared by
Steven L. Cobb
University of North Texas

Boston   Burr Ridge, IL   Dubuque, IA   Madison, WI   New York   San Francisco   St. Louis
Bangkok   Bogotá   Caracas   Lisbon   London   Madrid
Mexico City   Milan   New Delhi   Seoul   Singapore   Sydney   Taipei   Toronto

Irwin/McGraw-Hill
A Division of The McGraw-Hill Companies

Study Guide to accompany
INTERNATIONAL ECONOMICS

Copyright ©1998 by The McGraw-Hill Companies, Inc. All rights reserved.
Previous editions 1995, 1991 by Richard D. Irwin, Inc. Printed in the United States of America.
The contents of, or parts thereof, may be reproduced for use with
INTERNATIONAL ECONOMICS
Dennis R. Appleyard and Alfred J. Field
provided such reproductions bear copyright notice and may not be reproduced in
any form for any other purpose without permission of the publisher.

1 2 3 4 5 6 7 8 9 0 BBC/BBC 9 0 9 8 7

ISBN 0-256-17244-7

http://www.mhhe.com